GOURMET PUP

Homecooked Happiness

GOURMET PUP

Homecooked Happiness

Dana Wagtail

Copyright

NO PART OF THIS BOOK may be reproduced or transmitted in any form or by any means, electronic or mechanical, including photocopying, recording or any information storage or retrieval system without written permission from the author, except for the use of brief quotations in a book review or scholarly journal.

The author has made every effort to trace and acknowledge sources/resources/individuals.

In the event that any images/information have been incorrectly attributed or credited, the author will be pleased to rectify these omissions at the earliest opportunity.

Published By: Neuvare Books

Cover Design: Neuvare Books

Interior Layout and Design: Neuvare Books

For information regarding bulk purchases, special editions, book club editions, or licensing inquiries, please contact: books@neuvare.com

Visit the author's website at www.books.neuvare.com

First Edition: 2023
Copyright © 2023 Dana Wagtail
All rights reserved.
ISBN: 978-0-7961-4051-7

Disclaimer

THE CONTENT WITHIN THIS BOOK serves the sole purpose of providing general information and is intended for informational purposes only. It should not be considered a replacement for professional veterinary guidance, diagnosis, or treatment. For any inquiries about your pet's medical condition, it is imperative to consult your veterinarian or another qualified pet health provider. Your pet's well-being is of utmost importance, and seeking professional advice ensures that you make informed decisions regarding their health and nutrition.

The recipes included in this book have been carefully curated to offer a variety of nutritious options for your pets. However, pets may have specific dietary needs or allergies requiring specialised attention. It is crucial to consult with your veterinarian before making any significant changes to your pet's diet.

The authors and publishers of this book are not responsible for any adverse effects or consequences resulting from the use of the information contained herein. The recipes provided are meant to be used at the discretion and responsibility of the pet owner.

Furthermore, please ensure that all ingredients used in these recipes are fresh, safe and appropriate for your specific pet. Some pets may have sensitivities or allergies to certain foods, and it is imperative to be aware of any potential risks.

By using this book, you agree to release the authors and

publishers from any and all liability associated with the use of the information provided. You are responsible for exercising due diligence and taking appropriate precautions when preparing and feeding homemade pet food.

Always remember that the health and well-being of your pet should be your top priority. This book is a resource to help you make informed decisions about your pet's diet, but it is not a replacement for professional veterinary care.

Contents

Copyright 3
Disclaimer 4
Foreword 16
    Consult Your Veterinarian: 16
    Balanced Diet is Key: 16
    Allergies and Sensitivities: 17
    Hygiene and Food Safety: 17
    Quality Ingredients: 17
    Homemade Doesn't Mean Unregulated: 18
    Age-Appropriate Recipes: 18
    Treats vs Meals: 18
    Keep an Eye on Your Pet: 18
    The Joy of Cooking for Your Pets: 19

Introduction 20

Health and Well Being 21
    Dietary Needs 22
        Choose High-Quality Dog Food 22

Portion Control 24

Fresh Water Access.. 24

Balanced Diet... 25

Regular Feeding Schedule 25

Avoid Feeding Human Food............................... 25

Monitor for Allergies and Sensitivities.................. 25

Regular Exercise 26

Dental Care 26

Regular Vet Check-Ups 26

Grooming and Skin Care 27

Avoid Harmful Substances 27

Coconut Oil and Dogs.................................... 28

Understanding Coconut Oil: 28

Is Coconut Oil Safe for Dogs? 28

Potential Benefits for Dogs:................................. 29

Dangerous Foods 31

Foods to be aware of 32

Safe Foods 36

Striking a Balance 37

Low Sodium Broth 43

Introduction 44

Low-Sodium Beef Broth 1 45

Low-Sodium Beef Broth 2 49

Low-Sodium Chicken Broth 52

Low-Sodium Fish Broth 57

Low-Sodium Lamb Broth 61

Low-Sodium Pork Broth 64

Low-Sodium Vegetable Broth 68

Puppy Recipes 72

Introduction 73

Beef and Sweet Potato Stew 74

Beef and Pumpkin 75

Beef and Brown Rice 76

Beef and Oats 77

Chicken and Rice 78

Chicken and Sweet Potato 79

Chicken and Barley 80

Chicken and Millet 81

Chicken and Lentils 82

Salmon and Quinoa 83

Fish and Brown Rice 84

Salmon and Rice 85

Fish and Rice 86

Lamb and Quinoa 1 87

Lamb and Quinoa 2 88

Turkey and Brown Rice 89

Turkey and Oats 90

Turkey and Potato 91

Turkey and Sweet Potato 92

Turkey and Barley 93

Note 94

Adult Dog Recipes 95

Beef and Potato Hash 96

Beef and Sweet Potato Stew 97

Beef and Potato Casserole 98

Beef and Spinach Quiche 99

Beef and Zucchini Lasagne 100

Beef and Kale Stir-Fry 101

Beef and Spinach Omelette 102

Beef and Barley Medley 103

Beef and Veggie Stir-Fry 104

Beef and Quinoa Salad 105

Beef and Spinach Soup 106

Chicken and Rice Delight 107

Chicken and Pumpkin Soup 108
Chicken and Barley Risotto 109
Chicken and Pumpkin Pie 110
Chicken and Lentil Soup 111
Chicken and Carrot Omelette 112
Chicken and Rice Meatballs 113
Chicken and Butternut Squash Soup 114
Chicken and Potato Pancakes 115
Chicken and Cheese Pupcakes 116
Chicken and Brown Rice Meatloaf 117
Chicken and Potato Tacos 118
Chicken and Green Bean Casserole 119
Chicken and Rice Meatballs 120
Chicken and Barley Casserole 121
Chicken and Rice Burritos 122
Tuna and Spinach Pasta 123
Salmon and Potato Patties 125
Salmon and Asparagus Stir-Fry 126
Tuna and Carrot Muffins 127
Salmon and Sweet Potato Cakes 128
Tuna and Rice Salad 129
Salmon and Rice Medley 130
Tuna and Potato Salad 131

Tuna and Spinach Salad 132
Tuna and Spinach Wrap 133
Salmon and Rice Medley 134
Salmon and Carrot Omelette 135
Salmon and Quinoa Salad 136
Lamb and Rice Medley 137
Lamb and Barley Stew 138
Lamb and Pea Risotto 139
Lamb and Brown Rice Stew 140
Lamb and Rice Balls 141
Pork and Apple Casserole 142
Pork and Rice Stuffed Peppers 143
Pork and Rice Stir-Fry 144
Pork and Spinach Quiche 145
Pork and Carrot Stew 146
Pork and Apple Risotto 147
Pork and Barley Risotto 148
Pork and Sweet Potato Casserole 149
Pork and Potato Bake 150
Turkey and Quinoa Bowl 151
Turkey and Lentil Stew 153
Turkey and Rice Pilaf 154
Turkey and Broccoli Casserole 155

Turkey and Quinoa Stuffed Peppers 156

Turkey and Spinach Wraps 157

Turkey and Pumpkin Stew 158

Turkey and Pumpkin Stuffed Kong's 159

Turkey and Oatmeal Pancakes 160

Turkey and Rice Stuffed Tomatoes 161

Turkey and Sweet Potato Hash 162

Turkey and Carrot Stew 163

Turkey and Green Bean Stir-Fry 164

Turkey and Cranberry Balls 165

Veggie and Oatmeal Bake 166

Senior recipes 167

Introduction 168

Beef and Sweet Potato Stew: 169

Beef and Barley Stew: 170

Beef and Millet Stew: 171

Beef and Potato Casserole: 172

Chicken and Rice Delight: 173

Chicken and Sweet Potato Casserole: 174

Chicken and Potato Casserole: 175

Chicken and Lentil Stew: 176

Salmon and Asparagus Surprise: 177

Salmon and Quinoa Medley: 178
Salmon and Rice Delight: 179
Tuna and Brown Rice Medley: 180
Tuna and Lentil Medley: 181
Tuna and Oatmeal Delight: 182
Pork and Rice Medley: 183
Pork and Barley Medley: 184
Pork and Millet Medley: 185
Turkey and Brown Rice Surprise: 186
Turkey and Spinach Delight: 187
Turkey and Quinoa Surprise: 188

Treats 189
Beef and Potato Pancakes 190
Beef and Cheddar Biscuits 191
Beef and Cheese Dog Biscuits 192
Beef and Carrot Poppers 193
Beef and Potato Swirls 194
Beef and Sweet Potato Chews 195
Beef and Blueberry Chew Bars 196
Beef and Carrot Chews 197
Beef and Zucchini Chews 198
Chicken and Blueberry Bites 199

Chicken and Blueberry Chew Bars 200
Chicken and Brown Rice Chewie's 201
Chicken and Carrot Chew Strips 202
Chicken and Green Bean Chew Bars 203
Chicken and Pea Popsicles 205
Chicken and Carrot Pupcakes 206
Chicken and Sweet Potato Cookies 207
Chicken and Sweet Potato Squares 208
Chicken and Zucchini Biscuits 210
Salmon and Sweet Potato Dog Bites 211
Salmon and Sweet Potato Twists 212
Salmon and Quinoa Muffins 213
Salmon and Spinach Chew Bars 214
Salmon and Spinach Squares 216
Tuna and Spinach Chew Squares 217
Tuna and Spinach Chew Strips 219
Tuna and Spinach Drops 221
Tuna and Spinach Popsicles 222
Pork and Apple Cookies 223
Pork and Apple Chewies 224
Pork and Apple Doughnuts 225
Pork and Blueberry Chew Strips 226
Pork and Oatmeal Cookies 227

Pork and Sweet Potato Chew Strip 228

Pork and Pumpkin Chew Bars 229

Turkey and Broccoli Muffins 230

Turkey and Cranberry Dog Jerky 231

Turkey and Sweet Potato Dog Chews 232

Turkey and Cranberry Dog Bar 233

Turkey and Pumpkin Muffins 234

Turkey and Green Bean Chewie's 235

Turkey and Cranberry Chunks 236

Turkey and Spinach Chewie's 237

Turkey and Pumpkin Chew Bars 239

Veggie and Peanut Butter Dog Treats 240

Banana and Oatmeal Dog Treats 241

Pumpkin and Cinnamon Dog Biscuits 242

Blueberry and Banana Frozen Treats 243

Carrot and Apple Dog Cookies 244

Peanut Butter and Banana Frozen Treats 245

Blueberry and Yogurt Frozen Bites 246

Portion Sizes 247

Puppies 248

Adult Dogs 250

Senior Dogs 252

Foreword

BEFORE YOU EMBARK ON A culinary journey to prepare delectable homemade treats and meals for your beloved pets, it's essential to understand the importance of responsible pet nutrition. Our pet food recipes are designed to provide you with a wide array of creative and nutritious recipes that you can prepare in the comfort of your own kitchen. However, we would like to emphasise a few important points to ensure the health and well-being of your furry companions.

Consult Your Veterinarian:

While the recipes in this book are carefully crafted with the well-being of your pets in mind, it is imperative to consult your veterinarian before making any significant changes to your pet's diet. Every pet is unique, and their nutritional needs can vary based on their age, breed, and health condition. Your vet can offer valuable insights and guidance to help you tailor these recipes to your pet's specific requirements.

Balanced Diet is Key:

A balanced diet is crucial for your pet's overall health. While our recipes are designed to be nutritious, they should be a part of a well-rounded diet. Be mindful of the nutritional content of the meals you prepare and ensure they meet your pet's daily dietary requirements. Overfeeding or underfeeding can lead to health issues, so portion control is key.

Allergies and Sensitivities:

Pets, like humans, can have allergies and food sensitivities. Always be aware of any ingredients in the recipes that your pet may be allergic to. It's recommended to introduce new ingredients gradually and observe for any adverse reactions. If you notice any signs of allergies or sensitivities, discontinue the recipe and consult your vet immediately.

Hygiene and Food Safety:

Maintaining a clean and hygienic kitchen is essential when preparing food for your pets. Wash your hands and cooking utensils thoroughly before and after handling pet food ingredients. Store pet food safely, following the storage guidelines provided. Remember to separate pet food preparation from human food to prevent cross-contamination.

Quality Ingredients:

The quality of ingredients used in the recipes directly impacts the nutritional value of the meals. Always select fresh, high-quality ingredients and avoid using spoiled or expired products. When choosing meat, fish, or vegetables, ensure they are safe and suitable for pet consumption.

Homemade Doesn't Mean Unregulated:

It's important to note that homemade pet food does not go through the same regulatory processes as commercial pet food. While the recipes in this book are carefully crafted, it's essential to research the nutritional requirements for your specific pet and follow them diligently. Supplementing with commercial pet food or consulting with a veterinary nutritionist is advisable to ensure all essential nutrients are met.

Age-Appropriate Recipes:

Pets' dietary needs change as they age. It's crucial to provide age-appropriate meals for your pets. Puppies have different nutritional requirements than adult or senior pets. This recipe book offers a variety of options for all life stages, so choose recipes that align with your pet's age and growth stage.

Treats vs Meals:

Some recipes in this book are designed as treats and should not replace your pet's regular meals. While treats can be a fun and rewarding addition to your pet's diet, they should be given in moderation. Overindulgence in treats can lead to weight issues and an imbalanced diet.

Keep an Eye on Your Pet:

After introducing new recipes, keep a close watch on your pet's well-being. Monitor their behaviour, weight, coat condition, and overall health. If you notice any changes that concern you, consult your vet immediately.

The Joy of Cooking for Your Pets:

Preparing homemade pet food can be a deeply rewarding experience, fostering a stronger bond with your furry friends. With this book, we aim to provide you with a wide variety of options, that cater to your pet's taste and nutritional requirements. However, always remember that your pet's health and well-being should be the top priority.

The recipes in this book are crafted with love and care, but they should be part of a well-thought-out feeding plan that prioritises your pet's unique needs. Responsible pet nutrition, in consultation with your veterinarian, is the key to a happy and healthy life for your furry companions. Enjoy your culinary adventures, and may your pets savour every delightful bite!

Introduction

EMBARK ON A CULINARY CANINE JOURNEY WITH "GOURMET PUP"!

What sets " Gourmet Pup " apart is its commitment to making canine nutrition accessible and enjoyable for every pet parent. The recipes are easy to follow, even for those with minimal culinary experience, ensuring that you can create nutritious masterpieces in your own kitchen. The book is a celebration of the bond between you and your dog, transforming mealtime into a shared experience of joy and nourishment.

As you embark on this culinary journey, you'll discover the joy of preparing meals that go beyond the bowl – they become a gesture of love and care for your loyal companion. " Gourmet Pup " isn't just a cookbook; it's an invitation to create moments that will be etched in your dog's memory, one delicious recipe at a time.

So, why settle for store-bought when you can elevate your dog's dining experience to a whole new level? " Gourmet Pup " is more than a cookbook; it's a testament to the belief that our furry friends deserve the best. Treat your dog to the culinary adventure they deserve – because they're not just pets; they're family.

"Gourmet Pup" embodies a culinary experience that goes beyond mere sustenance for your furry friend. It creates a setting where each meal is a festive tribute to love, well-being, and enhances the sheer delight of living life as a dog.

Health and Well Being

Dietary Needs

Owning a pet dog is a rewarding experience that comes with the responsibility of ensuring their health and well-being. Just like humans, dogs require proper care and attention to thrive. One of the fundamental aspects of maintaining a healthy and happy dog is providing the right nutrition and meeting their dietary needs. In this book, we'll explore essential tips for taking care of your pet dog's health and dietary requirements.

Choose High-Quality Dog Food

The foundation of a dog's health begins with the food they consume. It's crucial to feed them high-quality dog food that meets their specific needs. When choosing food for your dog, consider the following:

- **Life Stage:** Dogs have different nutritional requirements at different stages of their lives. Puppies, adult dogs, and seniors all need tailored diets. Ensure that the food you feed them is appropriate for your dog's life stage.

- **Ingredients:** If supplementing with commercial food, check the ingredient list. Look for a protein source (like chicken, beef, or fish) as the main ingredient. Steer clear of foods that contain an abundance of fillers, preservatives, artificial additives, or by-products.

- **Home-cooked meals:** Feeding your dog home-cooked meals ensures that you know what they are eating. It guarantees the delivery of a personalised nutrition plan, ensuring your dog receives an optimal balance of proteins, fats, and carbohydrates. This approach aims to enhance overall well-being by incorporating thoughtfully chosen fresh ingredients.

- **Special Dietary Needs:** Providing home-cooked meals tailored to your dog's special dietary needs ensures precise nutrition, promoting overall health and addressing specific requirements that commercial diets may overlook. Enhance your dog's meals by incorporating vet-recommended supplements tailored to address their dietary requirements.

Portion Control

Overfeeding can lead to obesity, which can have severe health implications for your dog. Consult your veterinarian for guidance and follow their recommended portion sizes based on your dog's size and activity level. Be mindful not to give in to those pleading puppy eyes during mealtimes. Consult your veterinarian for guidance on portion control if you're uncertain.

Fresh Water Access

Proper hydration is essential for your dog's health. Ensure

that your furry companion always has access to a supply of fresh and clean water. Dehydration can lead to numerous health issues, so make sure the water bowl is regularly refilled.

Balanced Diet

A balanced diet is key to your dog's well-being. While dog food is formulated to contain all the necessary nutrients, you can also add some variety to their diet with occasional treats, fruits, and vegetables. Just ensure that the extra food is safe for dogs and doesn't constitute more than 10% of their daily calorie intake.

Regular Feeding Schedule

Ensuring your dog follows a consistent feeding routine is crucial to maintaining optimal digestive health. Most dogs do well with two meals a day, while puppies may require more frequent feedings. Stick to a consistent routine, and avoid free-feeding, which can make it difficult to monitor your dog's food intake.

Avoid Feeding Human Food

While it's tempting to share your meal scraps with your furry friend, many human foods are unsafe for dogs. Onions, chocolate, grapes, and foods high in salt or fat can be toxic to dogs. It's best to resist the urge and feed your dog only dog-safe treats.

Monitor for Allergies and Sensitivities

Keep an eye out for any signs of food allergies or sensitivities in your dog. Common symptoms include itching, gastrointestinal issues, or changes in behaviour. If you suspect your dog has food allergies, consult your veterinarian for guidance on an elimination diet or specialised food.

Regular Exercise

Diet alone is not enough to keep your dog healthy. Regular exercise is equally important. Engage your dog in physical activities like walks, runs, playtime, and interactive toys. Engaging in physical activity contributes to weight management and enhances cognitive stimulation.

Dental Care

Maintaining good oral health is frequently underestimated, yet it plays a pivotal role in ensuring the overall well-being of your canine companion. Dental problems can lead to other health issues. Brush your dog's teeth regularly and provide dental chews or toys that promote good oral hygiene.

Regular Vet Check-Ups

Regular appointments with a veterinarian are crucial for keeping tabs on your dog's overall well-being. Your vet can provide vaccinations, check for any underlying health conditions, and offer guidance on nutrition and preventative care. Depending on your dog's age and health, these check-ups may be needed annually or more frequently.

Grooming and Skin Care

Proper grooming and skin care are important for your dog's comfort and health. Regular brushing helps prevent matting, and it's an opportunity to check for ticks, fleas, or any skin issues. Bathing should be done as needed, but be cautious not to overdo it, as it can strip the natural oils from your dog's coat.

Avoid Harmful Substances

Be vigilant about substances that can harm your dog. Keep toxic plants, chemicals, and small objects that could be swallowed out of their reach. Dogs are known to be curious, so pet-proof your home just as you would for a child.

Taking care of your pet dog's health and dietary needs is a significant responsibility that comes with the joy of having a loyal companion. Providing high-quality food, proper portion control, regular exercise, and routine veterinary care are all vital elements of ensuring your dog's well-being.

By following these essential tips, you can help your furry friend live a long, healthy, and happy life.

Remember that each dog is unique, so it's important to tailor your care to their individual needs, and always consult with your veterinarian for specific guidance and recommendations.

Your canine bundle of fur will express gratitude through a joyful wag of the tail and an abundance of affection.

Coconut Oil and Dogs

The Canine Conundrum: Is Coconut Oil Safe for Dogs?

Pet owners often seek to enhance the well-being of their furry friends by incorporating various supplements into their diets. One such trending option is coconut oil.

Known for its potential health benefits in humans, many wonder whether coconut oil is a safe and beneficial addition to their canine companions' meals.

In this exploration, we will investigate the safety of incorporating coconut oil into your dogs' diets and uncover the potential benefits it might offer our canine companions.

Understanding Coconut Oil:

Coconut oil is derived from the flesh of coconuts and has gained popularity for its diverse applications in human nutrition and wellness. It contains a unique combination of fatty acids, including lauric acid, which is believed to have antimicrobial properties. Rich in medium-chain triglycerides (MCTs), coconut oil has been associated with various health benefits in humans, such as improved skin health, digestion, and potential antimicrobial effects.

Is Coconut Oil Safe for Dogs?

While coconut oil is generally considered safe for dogs when used **in moderation**, there are some important considerations to keep in mind:

1. **Moderation is Key:**

   Like any dietary supplement, moderation is crucial. Introducing coconut oil gradually and in small amounts allows you to monitor your dog's reaction and ensures that it doesn't upset their stomach.

2. **Caloric Content:**

   Coconut oil is calorie-dense, and excessive consumption may contribute to weight gain. It's essential to factor in the additional calories from coconut oil when planning your dog's overall diet.

3. **Allergies and Sensitivities:**

   Similar to humans, dogs may experience allergies or sensitivities to specific foods. Before introducing coconut oil, observe your dog for any signs of allergies or digestive issues. In the event of any negative reactions, it is advisable to promptly seek guidance from your veterinarian.

Potential Benefits for Dogs:

1. **Skin and Coat Health:**

   The MCTs in coconut oil may contribute to a glossy coat and healthy skin in dogs. Some pet owners report improvements in dry skin conditions or dull coats after incorporating coconut oil into their pets' diets.

2. Digestive Aid:

Coconut oil contains lauric acid, which has been associated with antimicrobial properties. In some cases, it might help promote digestive health and alleviate issues like constipation or diarrhoea.

3. Joint Health:

There is anecdotal evidence suggesting that the anti-inflammatory properties of coconut oil may benefit dogs with arthritis or joint issues. However, scientific studies in this regard are limited, and consultation with a veterinarian is advised.

So is coconut oil safe for your dog?

Coconut oil can be a safe and potentially beneficial addition to your dog's diet when used in moderation. While some pet owners report positive effects on their dogs' skin, coat, and overall well-being, individual responses may vary.

As with any dietary change, it's crucial to consult with your veterinarian before introducing coconut oil to your dog's meals, especially if your pet has pre-existing health conditions or is on a specific diet.

Remember, your dog's well-being is of the utmost importance, and any changes to their diet should be made with careful consideration of their individual needs and health status.

Dangerous Foods

Foods to be aware of

Understanding the potential harm that certain foods can pose to your canine companion is crucial for responsible pet ownership.

Here is a comprehensive list of foods that you should avoid giving to your dog to ensure their well-being:

1. Chocolate:

- The presence of theobromine and caffeine in chocolate renders it toxic to dogs.
- Symptoms include vomiting, diarrhoea, rapid breathing, and in severe cases, seizures or death.

2. Grapes and Raisins:

- Even small amounts can cause kidney failure in dogs.

3. Onions and Garlic:

- These contain compounds that can damage a dog's red blood cells, leading to anaemia.

4. Artificial Sweeteners:

- Xylitol, Sorbitol, and Mannitol, to name a few, can cause insulin release, leading to low blood sugar, seizures, and liver failure.

5. Alcohol:

- Affects dogs more rapidly than humans, even small amounts can be dangerous.

6. Bones:

- Cooked bones, especially from poultry, can splinter and cause choking or digestive tract damage.

7. Avocado:

- Contains persin, toxic to dogs; avoid the pit, skin, leaves, and even the flesh.

8. Macadamia Nuts:

- Known to cause weakness, tremors, vomiting, and increased body temperature.

9. Fatty Foods:

- Foods rich in fat have the potential to induce pancreatitis, a painful and potentially life-threatening inflammation of the pancreas.

10. Bread Dough:

- Raw dough can expand in the stomach, causing bloating, and the yeast can produce harmful alcohol.

11. Dairy Products:

- Many dogs are lactose intolerant, leading to digestive issues when consuming milk and cheese.

12. Caffeine:

- Found in coffee, tea, and energy drinks, can cause restlessness, rapid breathing, and death in dogs.

13. Salty Foods:

- Excessive salt intake can lead to sodium ion poisoning, with symptoms ranging from excessive thirst to seizures.

14. Fruit Pits and Seeds:

- Contain cyanide, which is toxic to dogs.

15. Mushrooms:

- Some mushrooms are dangerous to dogs, so it's best to avoid them altogether.

16. Raw Eggs:

- May contain harmful bacteria like Salmonella, leading to food poisoning in dogs.

17. Sugary Foods:

- High sugar intake can contribute to dental problems, obesity, and other health issues.

18. Spices:

- Certain spices, like garlic and nutmeg, can be harmful to dogs.

19. Human Medications:

- Many human medications are toxic to dogs, so keep them out of their reach.

20. Human Vitamins:

- Certain vitamins designed for humans can be toxic to dogs; ensure they are kept out of reach.

21. Canned Tuna (in Oil):

- High sodium content can lead to salt toxicity in dogs, and mercury levels can be harmful.

It is imperative to keep these foods inaccessible to your dog and refrain from sharing human food with them.

If you suspect your dog has ingested something toxic, promptly contact your veterinarian or an emergency animal clinic.

When uncertain, it's wise to err on the side of caution and consult your veterinarian for guidance on your dog's dietary needs and safe food options.

Responsible pet ownership includes being vigilant about what your furry friend consumes to ensure a long and healthy life.

Dana Wagtail

Safe Foods

Striking a Balance

The Key to a healthy diet is moderation

Feeding your dog, a well-balanced and nutritious diet, is crucial for their overall health and well-being.

You can include many of the foods listed in this book in your dog's diet, in *moderation*, but it's essential to be aware of potential risks and to introduce new items gradually.

Prior to making any substantial alterations to your dog's diet, it is advisable to seek guidance from your veterinarian..

Foods that are safe for dogs to eat.

1. **Apples**: *Remove seeds and core. Offer in moderation. Apples are a good source of vitamins.*

2. **Asparagus**: *Safe when cooked. One should offer asparagus in moderation as it is a source of vitamins.*

3. **Barley**: Like oats, barley is safe and can offer nutritional benefits. It's a wonderful source of fibre.

4. **Bell Peppers**: *Safe and rich in vitamins. Remove seeds and offer in moderation.*

5. **Blueberries**: Rich in antioxidants and safe for dogs. They can be a tasty and healthy treat.

6. **Broccoli**: *While broccoli is safe in small amounts, too much can cause stomach upset. Offer it cooked and in moderation.*

7. **Butternut Squash**: Safe and nutritious. Remove

seeds and cook before offering.

8. **Coconut Oil**: A small amount of coconut oil can be a healthy addition to your dog's food, providing beneficial fats.

9. **Carrots**: Excellent crunchy treats that are low in calories and high in vitamins. Raw or cooked carrots are both fine.

10. **Cottage Cheese**: *Like other dairy products, feed in moderation. Some dogs may be lactose intolerant.*

11. **Cranberries**: *In moderation, cranberries can be beneficial, especially for urinary tract health.*

12. **Cranberry Juice (Unsweetened):** Small amounts can be safe, but it's best to consult your vet. Too much acidity may upset your dog's stomach.

13. **Cucumber**: *Safe and low in calories. A refreshing treat in moderation.*

14. **Eggs**: A great source of protein. Ensure they are cooked thoroughly to avoid salmonella risk.

15. **Green Beans**: These are safe and low in calories. They can be a healthy addition to your dog's diet, either cooked or raw.

16. **Green Peas**: Rich in vitamins and safe for dogs. Incorporating peas into your dog's diet can contribute to their overall health and well-being.

17. **Kale**: *While rich in nutrients, kale contains oxalic acid. Offer it in moderation to avoid potential issues.*

Gourmet Pup

18. **Lentils:** High in protein and safe for dogs. Lentils can be a good addition to their diet.

19. **Low-Sodium Broth**: A small amount can be added to your dog's food for flavour. **Ensure that it is low in sodium.**

20. **Millet**: Safe for dogs and can provide essential nutrients. It's a gluten-free grain.

21. **Molasses**: While not toxic, it's high in sugar. Limit its use, as too much sugar can lead to health issues.

22. **Natural peanut butter**: *free from added sugars, salt, and other additives, can be a safe and tasty treat. Rich in healthy fats and protein, peanut butter can be an excellent source of energy for dogs. However, moderation is key due to its caloric density. Always check the label to ensure it doesn't contain xylitol, as sugar substitutes are toxic to dogs.*

23. **Oat Flour**: *A gluten-free alternative to traditional flours. Safe for dogs in moderation.*

24. **Oatmeal**: A healthy and digestible option for dogs. Avoid adding sugar or other sweeteners.

25. **Oats**: Oats are safe and can be a good source of fibre. They can offer particular advantages for dogs experiencing digestive concerns.

26. **Olive Oil**: A small amount of olive oil can be a healthy addition to your dog's food, providing beneficial fats.

27. **Pearl Barley**: Similar to regular barley, it's safe for

dogs and can offer nutritional value.

28. **Plain Yogurt**: An excellent source of probiotics. Ensure it's plain, unsweetened, and free from additives.

29. **Potatoes**: Safe when cooked but avoid feeding them raw. Sweet potatoes are a better option due to their nutritional content.

30. **Pumpkin**: A great source of fibre and can help with digestive issues. Ensure that it is natural, thoroughly cooked, and free from any additional sugars or spices.

31. **Quinoa**: A good source of protein and other nutrients. It's safe for dogs and can be included in their diet.

32. **Rice (Brown rice):** is a nutritious whole grain that can be a valuable component of a dog's diet. It serves as a valuable reservoir of dietary fibre, essential vitamins, and crucial minerals. When cooked thoroughly, brown rice is easily digestible for dogs, and its nutritional profile makes it a healthier choice than white rice. Incorporating brown rice into homemade dog meals can contribute to overall well-being.

33. **Rice (White Rice):** *White rice, though less nutrient-dense compared to brown rice, is still a safe option for dogs. It is easily digestible and can be beneficial during episodes of digestive upset or as a bland diet for dogs with sensitive stomachs. Like any food, it should be given in moderation to maintain a balanced diet for your pet.*

34. **Rice flour**: a common ingredient in many dog treats and foods, is generally safe for dogs. It is gluten-free, making it suitable for dogs with allergies or sensitivities to wheat. However, it's essential to ensure that rice flour is not the primary ingredient in your dog's diet, as it lacks the comprehensive nutritional profile found in whole grains.

35. **Spinach**: *Best served in moderation. While spinach contains beneficial nutrients, it also has oxalic acid, which can be harmful in large quantities.*

36. **Sweet Potato**: *Safe for dogs and a good source of vitamins and fibre. Ensure that it is cooked and offered in moderation.*

37. **Tomatoes**: *While ripe tomatoes are generally safe, green parts and stems contain solanine, which can be toxic. Offer in moderation.*

38. **Vegetable Oil**: In small amounts, vegetable oil is generally safe for dogs and can even provide essential fatty acids. It can be incorporated into their meals to enhance palatability and nutrient absorption.

39. **Whole Wheat Flour**: *While not harmful, it's best to feed dogs whole grains in moderation. Some dogs may be sensitive to wheat.*

40. **Whole Wheat Lasagne Noodles:** In moderation, plain and cooked noodles are safe for dogs.

41. **Whole Wheat Tortillas**: *In moderation, plain tortillas are safe for dogs. Avoid those with added spices or ingredients.*

42. **Zucchini**: Safe for dogs, either raw or cooked. It's a low-calorie option with some vitamins.

Maintaining a balanced and varied diet for your dog is essential for their health.

Ensure you follow recommended serving sizes and monitor your dog's reactions to new foods, consulting with your veterinarian for personalised advice.

Low Sodium Broth

Introduction

1. Portion Control: Consider freezing smaller portions of the broth for convenient serving. This allows you to defrost only what you need without wasting any of the delicious broth.

2. Introduce Gradually: If this is the first time you're introducing broth to your dog's diet, start with small amounts to ensure they tolerate it well.

3. Consult with Your Vet: Before making any significant changes to your dog's diet, especially if they have specific health concerns, it's always advisable to consult with your veterinarian.

4. Low in Sodium: By preparing the broth at home, you have control over the sodium content, ensuring it aligns with your dog's dietary needs.

Homemade broth is a wonderful way to add variety to your dog's meals while providing essential nutrients. Remember that moderation is key, and the broth should complement their regular balanced diet.

Low-Sodium Beef Broth 1

A Tasty and Healthy Treat for Your Canine Companion

Ingredients:

Beef Bones:

- Opt for high-quality, raw beef bones. These can be sourced from your local butcher or grocery store. The marrow-rich bones add flavour and nutrients to the broth.

Vegetables:

- 1 large carrot, washed and chopped
- 1 celery stalk, washed and chopped
- 1 sweet potato, washed and chopped
- These veggies not only enhance the taste but also contribute essential vitamins and minerals.

Herbs:

- A small handful of parsley
- 1 teaspoon of dried oregano
- Herbs bring additional flavour and potential health benefits.

Liquid Base:

- 10 cups of water
- Ensure your broth is hydrating by using a substantial amount of water.

Instructions:

1. **Prepare the Ingredients:**
    - Rinse the beef bones thoroughly under cold

water.

2. **Clean and chop the vegetables into bite-sized pieces.**
    - Tie the parsley into a small bundle using kitchen twine.

3. **Boil the Beef Bones:**
    - Place the beef bones in a large pot and cover them with water.
    - Bring the water to a boil and let it simmer for 10 minutes.
    - Discard the water to remove impurities.

4. **Combine Ingredients:**
    - Refill the pot with 10 cups of fresh water.
    - Add the cleaned and chopped vegetables, along with the bundled parsley and oregano.

5. **Simmer to Perfection:**
    - Bring the mixture to a boil, then reduce the Heat to a simmer.
    - Allow the broth to simmer for at least 2 hours, ensuring the flavours meld together.

6. **Strain and Cool:**
    - Once the broth has simmered to perfection, strain it to remove any solid particles.
    - Allow the broth to cool to room temperature before serving.

Serve in Moderation:

While this low-sodium beef broth is a healthy treat for your dog, moderation is key. Serve small amounts alongside their regular meals.

Health Benefits:

1. **Hydration:**
   - The broth provides an additional source of hydration, especially beneficial for dogs that may not drink enough water.

2. **Nutrient Boost:**
   - The combination of beef bones, vegetables, and herbs introduces various vitamins and minerals into your dog's diet.

3. **Joint Health:**
   - The marrow from the beef bones contains glucosamine, promoting joint health and mobility.

4. **Digestive Support:**
   - The gentle nature of broth can be soothing on your dog's digestive system.

Low-Sodium Beef Broth 2

Ingredients:

Beef Bones:

- 1 lb beef marrow bones (ensure they are pet-safe and free from seasoning)

Vegetables:

- 1 carrot, chopped
- 1/2 cup pumpkin, cubed

- 1/4 cup green peas
- 1/4 cup butternut squash, diced

Herbs:

- 1 sprig of catnip (optional)
- 1 tablespoon dried cat thyme (cat-safe variety)
- 1 tablespoon parsley, finely chopped

Liquid Base:

- 6 cups water

Instructions:

1. **Preparation of Beef Bones:**
   - Start by preheating your oven to 400°F (200°C). Place the beef marrow bones on a baking sheet and roast them in the oven for approximately 30 minutes. This roasting process enhances the flavour of the broth.

2. **Vegetable Preparation:**
   - While the bones are roasting, chop the carrot, pumpkin, and butternut squash into small, dog-sized pieces. These vegetables not only add flavour but also contribute essential nutrients.

3. **Boiling the Bones:**
   - Transfer the roasted bones to a large pot and cover them with 6 cups of water. Bring the water to a gentle boil and then reduce the

Heat to a simmer. Allow the bones to simmer for about 1-2 hours, extracting the rich flavours.

4. **Adding Vegetables:**
    - After the bones have simmered, add the chopped vegetables to the pot. Continue simmering for an additional 20-30 minutes until the vegetables are tender but not mushy.

5. **Introducing Herbs:**
    - Add the cat-safe herbs – catnip, dried cat thyme, and chopped parsley – to the pot. These herbs not only appeal to your cat's senses but also provide additional health benefits.

6. **Cooling and Straining:**
    - Once the broth has absorbed all the flavours, remove the pot from Heat and let it cool to room temperature. Strain the broth to remove bones and vegetable pieces, leaving only the liquid.

7. **Storing the Broth:**
    - Pour the strained broth into dog-safe containers and store them in the refrigerator for up to a week. Alternatively, freeze the broth in ice cube trays for convenient portioning.

8. **Serving Size:**
    - Before serving, warm the broth slightly to room temperature. Pour it over your dog's regular food or offer it as a standalone treat. Always observe your dog's response to new foods and adjust the serving size accordingly.

Low-Sodium Chicken Broth

Ingredients:

Chicken Meat & Bones:

- 2 pounds of chicken (preferably lean meat)

Vegetables:

- 1 cup of carrots, chopped
- 1 cup of green beans, chopped
- 1 cup of pumpkin, diced

Herbs:

- 1 teaspoon of turmeric (optional, for its anti-inflammatory properties)

Liquid Base:

- 4 cups of water
- 1 tablespoon of olive oil

Instructions:

1. **Prepare the Chicken:**
   - Trim excess fat from the chicken, ensuring you use lean meat.

2. **Cooking the Broth:**
   - In a large pot, Heat the olive oil over medium Heat.
   - Add the chicken pieces and cook until they are browned on all sides.

3. **Vegetable Addition:**
   - Add the chopped carrots, green beans, and

- diced pumpkin to the pot.
- Stir the vegetables and chicken together, allowing them to cook for an additional minute..

4. **Water and Simmering:**
   - Pour in the water, ensuring it covers the ingredients.
   - Bring the mixture to a boil, then reduce the Heat to a simmer.

5. **Seasoning:**
   - If you choose to use turmeric, add it to the broth at this point.
   - Simmer the broth for at least 30-45 minutes, allowing the flavours to meld.

6. **Cooling and Straining:**
   - Allow the broth to cool to room temperature.
   - Strain the broth to remove any bones or vegetable pieces, ensuring a smooth liquid.

7. **Storage:**
   - Once strained, store the broth in airtight containers.
   - Refrigerate for up to five days or freeze in portions for a longer shelf life.

Nutritional Benefits:

1. **Protein-Rich Chicken:**
   - Chicken provides essential proteins that contribute to muscle development and overall health.

2. **Nutrient-Packed Vegetables:**
   - Carrots offer beta-carotene, promoting good vision.
   - Green beans provide fibre and various vitamins.
   - Pumpkin is rich in fibre and aids in digestion.

3. **Low-Sodium Option:**
   - This homemade broth allows you to control the sodium content, ensuring it aligns with your dog's dietary needs.

4. **Anti-Inflammatory Turmeric:**
   - Turmeric, if included, brings anti-inflammatory properties that can benefit your dog's joint health.

Important Considerations:

1. **Consult Your Vet:**
   - Before introducing any new food into your dog's diet, consult with your veterinarian to ensure it aligns with their specific health

needs.

2. **Portion Control:**
    - While this broth is a healthy addition, moderation is key. Adjust serving sizes based on your dog's size and dietary requirements.

3. **Check for Allergies:**
    - Monitor your dog for any allergic reactions after introducing the broth. Discontinue use if any adverse effects occur.

Low-Sodium Fish Broth

Ingredients:

Fish Heads & Bones:

- 2 pounds of fish heads and bones (ensure they are deboned for safety)

Vegetables:

- 1 large sweet potato, peeled and chopped

- 2 carrots, washed and sliced
- 1 zucchini, diced
- 1 cup green beans, chopped

Herbs:

- 1 tablespoon dried parsley

Liquid Base:

- 8 cups water
- 1 tablespoon olive oil

Instructions:

1. **Prepare the Fish Heads and Bones:**
   - Make sure the fish heads and bones are thoroughly cleaned and deboned. Remove any sharp or small bones that may pose a choking hazard to your dog.

2. **Vegetable Preparation:**
   - Peel and chop the sweet potato into small pieces.
   - Wash and slice the carrots.
   - Dice the zucchini and chop the green beans.

3. **Sauté the Vegetables:**
   - In a large pot, Heat olive oil over medium Heat.

- Add the sweet potato, carrots, zucchini, and green beans. Sauté for 5 minutes until the vegetables start to soften.

4. **Add Fish Heads and Bones:**
   - Place the cleaned fish heads and bones into the pot with sautéed vegetables.

5. **Pour in Water:**
   - Add 8 cups of water to the pot. Ensure that the ingredients are well-covered with water.

6. **Bring to a Boil and Simmer:**
   - Bring the mixture to a boil, then reduce the Heat to a simmer. Allow it to simmer for about 45-60 minutes. This slow simmering helps extract the flavours from the fish and vegetables.

7. **Add Dried Parsley:**
   - Sprinkle dried parsley into the broth. Parsley not only adds a hint of flavour but also offers additional nutrients.

8. **Strain the Broth:**
   - Once the broth has simmered and the flavours have melded, strain the mixture to remove any bones, fish parts, and vegetable remnants.

9. **Cool and Store:**
   - Allow the broth to cool completely before

transferring it into storage containers. Refrigerate or freeze the broth based on your dog's consumption rate.

10. Serve in Moderation:

- Introduce the fish broth to your dog's diet in moderation. You can add it to their regular meals or serve it as an occasional treat.

Benefits of Homemade Fish Broth for Dogs:

1. Rich in Nutrients:

- Fish is a great source of omega-3 fatty acids, which contribute to a healthy coat and skin for your dog.

2. Joint Health:

- The natural gelatine from fish bones supports joint health, making this broth beneficial for dogs, especially those with arthritis or joint issues.

3. Hydration:

- Broths are an excellent way to keep your dog hydrated, especially if they are not keen on drinking plain water.

4. Low in Sodium:

- By preparing the broth at home, you have control over the sodium content, ensuring it aligns with your dog's dietary needs.

Low-Sodium Lamb Broth

Ingredients:

Lamb Bones:

- 1 pound lamb bones or lamb shanks

Vegetables:

- 2 carrots, chopped
- 2 celery stalks, chopped

- 1 sweet potato, peeled and diced
- 1 cup green beans, chopped

Herbs:

- 1 teaspoon dried rosemary
- 1 teaspoon dried parsley
- 1/2 teaspoon turmeric (optional)

Liquid Base:

- 2 quarts water
- 1 tablespoon olive oil

Instructions:

1. **Prepare the Lamb Bones:**
   - If you're using lamb shanks, place them in a large pot and cover with water. Bring to a boil, then reduce Heat and simmer for 15 minutes. Drain and rinse the bones under cool water to remove any impurities.

2. **Sauté the Vegetables:**
   - In the same pot, Heat olive oil over medium Heat. Add chopped carrots, celery, sweet potato, and green beans. Sauté for 5-7 minutes until the vegetables begin to soften.

3. **Add Lamb Bones and Water:**

- Place the lamb bones back into the pot with the sautéed vegetables. Pour in 2 quarts of water, ensuring the bones and vegetables are fully submerged.

4. **Season the Broth:**
   - Add dried rosemary, parsley, and turmeric (if using) to the pot. These herbs not only enhance the flavour but also offer additional health benefits for your dog.

5. **Simmer to Perfection:**
   - Bring the mixture to a boil, then reduce the heat to low. Allow the broth to simmer for 2-3 hours. This slow-cooking process extracts the flavours from the bones and vegetables, creating a rich and nutritious broth.

6. **Strain the Broth:**
   - Once the broth has simmered to perfection, strain it to remove bones and vegetable remnants. Use a fine mesh strainer or cheesecloth to ensure a clear and smooth broth.

7. **Cool and Store:**
   - Let the broth cool to room temperature before storing it. Once cooled, you can portion it into airtight containers or ice cube trays for easy serving. Refrigerate for up to a week or freeze for longer storage.

Low-Sodium Pork Broth

Ingredients:

Pork Bones:

- 1 pound lean pork bones

Vegetables:

- 2 carrots, chopped

- 2 celery stalks, chopped
- 1 sweet potato, peeled and diced
- 1 zucchini, sliced

Herbs:

- 1 teaspoon turmeric
- 1 teaspoon dried parsley
- 1 teaspoon dried rosemary

Liquid Base:

- 8 cups water
- 1 tablespoon apple cider vinegar

Instructions:

1. **Prepare the Pork Bones:**
   - Start by obtaining lean pork bones from your local butcher. Rinse them thoroughly under cold water to remove any impurities.

2. **Vegetable Medley:**
   - In a large pot, combine the chopped carrots, celery, sweet potato, and zucchini. These vegetables not only add flavour but also contribute essential vitamins and minerals to the broth.

3. **Add the Pork Bones:**
   - Place the cleaned pork bones into the pot with the vegetables. The combination of bones and vegetables forms the base of a nutritious broth.

4. **Pour in Water:**
   - Add 8 cups of water to the pot, covering the ingredients. This ratio ensures a rich and flavourful broth

5. **Enhance with Flavours:**
   - Incorporate apple cider vinegar, turmeric, dried parsley, and dried rosemary into the mix. These ingredients not only enhance the taste but also provide additional health benefits for your dog.

6. **Simmer to Perfection:**
   - Bring the mixture to a boil and then reduce the Heat to a simmer. Allow it to simmer for at least 2-3 hours. This slow-cooking process extracts all the goodness from the bones and vegetables.

7. **Strain and Cool:**
   - Once the broth has simmered to perfection, strain the liquid to remove bones and vegetable remnants. Let it cool to room temperature before storing.

8. **Storage:**
    - Portion the broth into airtight containers or ice cube trays for convenient serving sizes. Refrigerate or freeze based on your dog's consumption rate.

Health Benefits:

1. **Joint Health:**
    - The natural gelatine extracted from the pork bones during the simmering process promotes joint health and can be particularly beneficial for older dogs.

2. **Digestive Aid:**
    - The apple cider vinegar aids digestion, while the vegetables contribute fibre, promoting a healthy digestive system.

3. **Anti-Inflammatory Properties:**
    - Turmeric, known for its anti-inflammatory properties, can be beneficial for dogs with arthritis or joint inflammation.

4. **Hydration:**
    - The broth's enticing flavour encourages dogs to consume more liquids, aiding in overall hydration.

Dana Wagtail

Low-Sodium Vegetable Broth

This homemade vegetable broth serves as a tasty addition to your dog's meals while providing essential nutrients.

Gourmet Pup

Ingredients:

Vegetables:

- 2 large carrots, chopped
- 1 cup sweet potatoes, diced
- 1 cup green beans, chopped
- 1 cup peas
- 1 zucchini, sliced
- 1 celery stalk, chopped

Herbs:

- 1 sprig of fresh rosemary
- 2-3 sprigs of fresh parsley
- 1 tablespoon dried basil
- 1 tablespoon dried oregano

Grains:

- 1/2 cup brown rice or quinoa (optional)

Liquid Base:

- 8 cups water

Instructions:

1. **Prepare the Vegetables:**
   - Start by washing and chopping all the vegetables. Ensure they are cut into bite-sized pieces suitable for your dog's consumption.

2. **Adding Vegetables:**
   - Add the chopped carrots, sweet potatoes, green beans, peas, zucchini, and celery to the pot. Stir the vegetables for a few minutes, allowing them to slightly soften.

3. **Introducing Herbs:**
   - Tie the rosemary and parsley sprigs together with kitchen twine. Add this herb bundle, along with the dried basil and oregano, to the pot. Herbs not only enhance the flavour but also contribute beneficial nutrients.

4. **Incorporating Grains (Optional):**
   - If you choose to include grains in your dog's broth, add brown rice or quinoa to the pot. These grains add texture and additional nutrients to the broth.

5. **Pouring in Liquid:**
   - Pour in 8 cups of water. Bring the mixture to a boil, then reduce the Heat to simmer. Let it cook for about 30-40 minutes to allow the flavours to meld.

6. **Cooling and Straining:**
   - Once the broth has simmered to perfection, remove it from Heat and let it cool. Once it reaches room temperature, strain the broth to remove solid pieces, ensuring you retain only the liquid.

7. **Storing the Broth:**
   - Transfer the broth into airtight containers. You can store it in the refrigerator for up to a week or freeze it for longer shelf life. Make sure to label the containers with the date for easy tracking.

8. **Serving Size:**
   - When serving, warm the broth slightly and pour it over your dog's regular food. Ensure it's at a temperature that won't burn their mouth, and always monitor their response to new foods.

Dana Wagtail

Puppy Recipes

Introduction

Providing nutritious meals for a growing puppy is essential for their health and development. Here are home-cooked meal recipes for your puppy. Each recipe is designed to cater to one puppy.

Consult your veterinarian before using these recipes to ensure they are suitable for your puppy's dietary needs.

Dana Wagtail

Beef and Sweet Potato Stew

Ingredients:

- 100g (3.5 oz) lean ground beef
- 1/2 cup sweet potatoes (cooked and mashed)
- 1/4 cup green beans (cooked and chopped)

Steps:

1. Brown the ground beef in a pan until fully cooked.
2. Cook and mash the sweet potatoes.
3. Steam the green beans until tender.
4. Mix all the ingredients and serve.

Cooking Time: 20 minutes

Cooking Temperature: Medium Heat

Beef and Pumpkin

Ingredients:

- 100g (3.5 oz) lean ground beef
- 1/2 cup pumpkin (cooked and mashed)
- 1/4 cup spinach[i] (cooked and chopped)

Steps:

1. Brown the ground beef in a pan until fully cooked.
2. Cook and mash the pumpkin.
3. Steam the spinach until tender.
4. Mix all the ingredients and serve.

Cooking Time: 20 minutes

Cooking Temperature: Medium Heat

---

[i] *Spinach contains beneficial nutrients, it also has oxalic acid, which can be harmful in large quantities.*

Dana Wagtail

Beef and Brown Rice

Ingredients:

- 100g (3.5 oz) lean ground beef
- 1/2 cup brown rice (cooked)
- 1/4 cup green peas (cooked)

Steps:

1. Brown the ground beef in a pan until fully cooked.
2. Cook the brown rice according to package Steps.
3. Cook the green peas until they are soft.
4. Mix all the ingredients and serve.

Cooking Time: 20 minutes

Cooking Temperature: Medium Heat

Beef and Oats

Ingredients:

- 100g (3.5 oz) lean ground beef
- 1/2 cup oats (cooked)
- 1/4 cup zucchini (cooked and chopped)

Steps:

1. Brown the ground beef in a pan until fully cooked.
2. Cook the oats according to package Steps.
3. Steam the zucchini until it's soft.
4. Mix all the ingredients and serve.

Cooking Time: 20 minutes

Cooking Temperature: Medium Heat

Chicken and Rice

Ingredients:

- 100g (3.5 oz) boneless chicken breast
- 1/2 cup white rice (cooked)
- 1/4 cup carrots (steamed and chopped)

Steps:

1. Cook the chicken breast thoroughly, then chop it into small pieces.
2. Cook the rice according to package Steps.
3. Steam the carrots until they're tender.
4. Mix all the ingredients and serve.

Cooking Time: 20 minutes

Cooking Temperature: Medium Heat

Chicken and Sweet Potato

Ingredients:

- 100g (3.5 oz) Boneless chicken thighs
- 1/2 cup sweet potatoes (cooked and mashed)
- 1/4 cup green peas (cooked)

Steps:

1. Cook the chicken thighs thoroughly.
2. Chop meat it into small pieces.
3. Cook and mash the sweet potatoes.
4. Cook the green peas until soft.
5. Mix all the ingredients and serve.

Cooking Time: 20 minutes

Cooking Temperature: Medium Heat

If using chicken thighs on the bone[ii].

Remove all the cooked meat and ensure that all bones have been removed.

[ii] Cooked bones, especially from poultry, can splinter and cause choking or digestive tract damage.

Dana Wagtail

Chicken and Barley

Ingredients:

- 100g (3.5 oz) boneless chicken breast
- 1/2 cup barley (cooked)
- 1/4 cup broccoli (steamed and chopped)

Steps:

1. Cook the chicken breast thoroughly, then chop it into small pieces.
2. Cook the barley according to package Steps.
3. Steam the broccoli until it's tender.
4. Mix all the ingredients and serve.

Cooking Time: 20 minutes

Cooking Temperature: Medium Heat

Chicken and Millet

Ingredients:

- 100g (3.5 oz) boneless chicken breast
- 1/2 cup millet (cooked)
- 1/4 cup spinach[iii] (cooked and chopped)

Steps:

1. Cook the chicken breast thoroughly, then chop it into small pieces.
2. Cook the millet according to package Steps.
3. Steam the spinach until it's tender.
4. Mix all the ingredients and serve.

Cooking Time: 20 minutes

Cooking Temperature: Medium Heat

[iii] *Spinach contains beneficial nutrients, it also has oxalic acid, which can be harmful in large quantities.*

Dana Wagtail

Chicken and Lentils

Ingredients:

- 100g (3.5 oz) boneless chicken breast
- 1/2 cup cooked lentils
- 1/4 cup peas (cooked)

Steps:

1. Cook the chicken breast thoroughly, then chop it into small pieces.
2. Cook the lentils according to package Steps.
3. Cook the peas until they are soft.
4. Mix all the ingredients and serve.

Cooking Time: 20 minutes

Cooking Temperature: Medium Heat

Salmon and Quinoa

Ingredients:

- 100g (3.5 oz) salmon fillet
- 1/2 cup quinoa (cooked)
- 1/4 cup broccoli (steamed and chopped)

Steps:

1. Bake or steam the salmon until it flakes easily.
2. Cook the quinoa according to package Steps.
3. Steam the broccoli until it's tender.
4. Mix all the ingredients and serve.

Cooking Time: 20 minutes

Cooking Temperature: Medium Heat

Fish and Brown Rice

Ingredients:

- 100g (3.5 oz) white fish fillet (e.g., tilapia[iv])
- 1/2 cup brown rice (cooked)
- 1/4 cup carrots (steamed and chopped)

Steps:

1. Bake or steam the fish until it flakes easily.
2. Cook the brown rice according to package Steps.
3. Steam the carrots until they're tender.
4. Mix all the ingredients and serve.

Cooking Time: 20 minutes

Cooking Temperature: Medium Heat

[iv] Cooked bones can splinter and cause choking or digestive tract damage.

Salmon and Rice

Ingredients:

- 100g (3.5 oz) salmon fillet
- 1/2 cup white rice (cooked)
- 1/4 cup peas (cooked)

Steps:

1. Bake or steam the salmon until it flakes easily.
2. Cook the white rice according to package Steps.
3. Cook the peas until they are soft.
4. Mix all the ingredients and serve.

Cooking Time: 20 minutes

Cooking Temperature: Medium Heat

Dana Wagtail

Fish and Rice

Ingredients:

- 100g (3.5 oz) white fish fillet (e.g., tilapia[v])
- 1/2 cup white rice (cooked)
- 1/4 cup spinach[vi] (cooked and chopped)

Steps:

1. Bake or steam the fish until it flakes easily.
2. Cook the white rice according to package Steps.
3. Steam the spinach until it's tender.
4. Mix all the ingredients and serve.

Cooking Time: 20 minutes

Cooking Temperature: Medium Heat

---

[v] Cooked bones can splinter and cause choking or digestive tract dam

[vi] *Spinach contains beneficial nutrients, it also has oxalic acid, which can be harmful in large quantities.*

Lamb and Quinoa 1

Ingredients:

- 100g (3.5 oz) ground lamb
- 1/2 cup quinoa (cooked)
- 1/4 cup green beans (cooked and chopped)

Steps:

1. Cook the ground lamb until browned and fully cooked.
2. Cook the quinoa according to package Steps.
3. Steam the green beans until tender.
4. Mix all the ingredients and serve.

Cooking Time: 20 minutes

Cooking Temperature: Medium Heat

Dana Wagtail

Lamb and Quinoa 2

Ingredients:

- 100g (3.5 oz) ground lamb
- 1/2 cup quinoa (cooked)
- 1/4 cup carrots (steamed and chopped)

Steps:

1. Cook the ground lamb until browned and fully cooked.
2. Cook the quinoa according to package Steps.
3. Steam the carrots until they're tender.
4. Mix all the ingredients and serve.

Cooking Time: 20 minutes

Cooking Temperature: Medium Heat

Turkey and Brown Rice

Ingredients:

- 100g (3.5 oz) ground turkey
- 1/2 cup brown rice (cooked)
- 1/4 cup peas (cooked)

Steps:

1. Cook the ground turkey until browned and fully cooked.
2. Cook the brown rice according to package Steps.
3. Cook the peas until they are soft.
4. Mix all the ingredients and serve.

Cooking Time: 20 minutes

Cooking Temperature: Medium Heat

Turkey and Oats

Ingredients:

- 100g (3.5 oz) ground turkey
- 1/2 cup oats (cooked)
- 1/4 cup zucchini (cooked and chopped)

Steps:

1. Cook the ground turkey until browned and fully cooked.
2. Cook the oats according to package Steps.
3. Steam the zucchini until it's soft.
4. Mix all the ingredients and serve.

Cooking Time: 20 minutes

Cooking Temperature: Medium Heat

Turkey and Potato

Ingredients:

- 100g (3.5 oz) ground turkey
- 1/2 cup potatoes (cooked and mashed)
- 1/4 cup carrots (steamed and chopped)

Steps:

1. Cook the ground turkey until browned and fully cooked.
2. Cook and mash the potatoes.
3. Steam the carrots until they're tender.
4. Mix all the ingredients and serve.

Cooking Time: 20 minutes

Cooking Temperature: Medium Heat

Dana Wagtail

Turkey and Sweet Potato

Ingredients:

- 100g (3.5 oz) ground turkey
- 1/2 cup sweet potatoes (cooked and mashed)
- 1/4 cup green beans (cooked and chopped)

Steps:

1. Cook the ground turkey until browned and fully cooked.
2. Cook and mash the sweet potatoes.
3. Steam the green beans until they're tender.
4. Mix all the ingredients and serve.

Cooking Time: 20 minutes

Cooking Temperature: Medium Heat

Turkey and Barley

Ingredients:

- 100g (3.5 oz) ground turkey
- 1/2 cup barley (cooked)
- 1/4 cup broccoli (steamed and chopped)

Steps:

1. Cook the ground turkey until browned and fully cooked.
2. Cook the barley according to package Steps.
3. Steam the broccoli until it's tender.
4. Mix all the ingredients and serve.

Cooking Time: 20 minutes

Cooking Temperature: Medium Heat

Note

Remember to let the meals cool before serving them to your puppy, and always consult with your veterinarian to ensure these recipes are suitable for your puppy's specific dietary needs. These recipes offer a variety of proteins and grains to keep your puppy happy and healthy.

Enjoy cooking for your furry friend!

Gourmet Pup

Adult Dog Recipes

Beef and Potato Hash

Ingredients:

- 2 cups (475 ml) lean ground beef
- 1 cup (200 g) potatoes, diced
- 1/2 cup (75 g) green beans, chopped
- 1/4 cup (60 ml) water

Steps:

1. Brown ground beef in a skillet.
2. Add diced potatoes, green beans, and water.
3. Cook until potatoes are tender.

Cooking Time: 20 minutes

Cooking Temperature: Medium Heat.

Beef and Sweet Potato Stew

Ingredients:

- 2 cups (475 ml) lean ground beef
- 1 cup (200 g) sweet potatoes, diced
- 1/2 cup (75 g) green peas
- 1/4 cup (60 g) carrots, sliced
- 2 cups (475 ml) water

Steps:

1. Brown the ground beef in a pan.
2. Add sweet potatoes, carrots, peas, and water.
3. Simmer until vegetables are tender.

Cooking Time: 30 minutes

Cooking Temperature: Medium Heat.

Dana Wagtail

Beef and Potato Casserole

Ingredients:

- 2 cups (475 ml) lean ground beef
- 1 cup (200 g) potatoes, diced
- 1/2 cup (75 g) green beans, chopped
- 1/4 cup (60 ml) water

Steps:

1. Brown ground beef in a skillet.
2. Add diced potatoes, green beans, and water.
3. Bake at 375°F (190°C) for 25 minutes.

Cooking Time: 25 minutes

Cooking Temperature: 375°F (190°C)

Beef and Spinach Quiche

Ingredients:

- 2 cups (475 ml) lean ground beef
- 1 cup (240 g) spinach[vii], chopped
- 1/2 cup (75 g) low-fat cottage cheese
- 1/4 cup (60 g) oats
- 2 eggs

Steps:

1. Brown ground beef in a skillet.
2. Mix in chopped spinach, cottage cheese, oats, and eggs.
3. Bake at 375°F (190°C) for 25 minutes.

Cooking Time: 25 minutes

Cooking Temperature: 375°F (190°C)

[vii] Spinach is b*est served in moderation. While spinach contains beneficial nutrients, it also has oxalic acid, which can be harmful in large quantities.*

Dana Wagtail

Beef and Zucchini Lasagne

Ingredients:

- 2 cups (475 ml) lean ground beef
- 1 cup (240 g) zucchini, sliced
- 1/2 cup (75 g) whole wheat lasagne noodles, cooked
- 1/4 cup (60 g) low-sodium beef broth

Steps:

1. Brown ground beef in a skillet.
2. Add sliced zucchini, cooked whole wheat lasagne noodles, and beef broth.
3. Layer like a lasagne and bake at 375°F (190°C) for 30 minutes.

Cooking Time: 30 minutes

Cooking Temperature: 375°F (190°C)

Beef and Kale Stir-Fry

Ingredients:

- 2 cups (475 ml) lean ground beef
- 1 cup (240 g) kale[viii], chopped
- 1/2 cup (75 g) brown rice, cooked

Steps:

1. Brown ground beef in a skillet.
2. Add chopped kale, and cooked brown rice
3. Stir-fry until Heated through.

Cooking Time: 15 minutes

Cooking Temperature: Medium Heat

[viii] *While rich in nutrients, kale contains oxalic acid. Offer it in moderation to avoid potential issues.*

Dana Wagtail

Beef and Spinach Omelette

Ingredients:

- 2 cups (475 ml) lean ground beef
- 1 cup (240 g) fresh spinach[ix], chopped
- 2 eggs
- 1/4 cup (60 ml) low-sodium beef broth

Steps:

1. Brown ground beef in a skillet.
2. Mix in chopped spinach and low-sodium beef broth.
3. Cook as you would an omelette with the eggs.

Cooking Time: 10 minutes

Cooking Temperature: Medium Heat.

[ix] Spinach is b*est served in moderation. While spinach contains beneficial nutrients, it also has oxalic acid, which can be harmful in large quantities.*

Beef and Barley Medley

Ingredients:

- 2 cups (475 ml) lean ground beef
- 1 cup (185 g) pearl barley
- 1/2 cup (75 g) green peas
- 1/4 cup (60 g) carrots, finely chopped
- 2 cups (475 ml) low-sodium beef broth

Steps:

1. Brown ground beef in a pot.
2. Add pearl barley, green peas, carrots, and low-sodium beef broth.
3. Simmer until the medley thickens and is Heated through.

Cooking Time: 20 minutes

Cooking Temperature: Low Heat.

Beef and Veggie Stir-Fry

Ingredients:

- 2 cups (475 ml) lean ground beef
- 1 cup (185 g) broccoli florets
- 1/2 cup (75 g) sweet potatoes, diced and cooked
- 1/4 cup (60 g) carrots, finely chopped
- 1/4 cup (60 ml) low-sodium beef broth

Steps:

1. Brown ground beef in a skillet.
2. Add broccoli, cooked sweet potatoes, carrots, and low-sodium beef broth.
3. Stir-fry until heated through.

Cooking Time: 20 minutes

Cooking Temperature: Medium Heat.

Beef and Quinoa Salad

Ingredients:

- 2 cups (475 ml) lean ground beef
- 1 cup (185 g) cooked quinoa
- 1/2 cup (75 g) cucumber, diced
- 1/4 cup (60 g) low-sodium beef broth

Steps:

1. Brown ground beef in a skillet.
2. Mix in cooked quinoa, diced cucumber, and low-sodium beef broth.
3. Serve as a salad.

Cooking Time: 20 minutes

Cooking Temperature: Medium Heat.

Dana Wagtail

Beef and Spinach Soup

Ingredients:

- 2 cups (475 ml) lean ground beef
- 1 cup (240 g) fresh spinach[x] leaves
- 1/2 cup (75 g) white rice, cooked
- 1/4 cup (60 ml) low-sodium beef broth

Steps:

1. Brown the ground beef in a skillet.
2. Add fresh spinach leaves, cooked white rice, and low-sodium beef broth.
3. Simmer until the soup is heated through.

Cooking Time: 20 minutes

Cooking Temperature: Medium Heat.

---

[x] Spinach is b*est served in moderation. While spinach contains beneficial nutrients, it also has oxalic acid, which can be harmful in large quantities.*

Chicken and Rice Delight

Ingredients:

- 2 cups (475 ml) Boneless chicken breast, cooked and shredded
- 1 cup (240 g) brown rice, cooked
- 1/2 cup (75 g) carrots, diced
- 1/4 cup (60 g) peas
- 1/4 cup (60 g) green beans, chopped
- 1 tablespoon (15 ml) olive oil

Steps:

1. Cook chicken and rice separately.
2. Sauté carrots, peas, and green beans in olive oil until tender.
3. Mix all ingredients and let cool before serving.

Cooking Time: 20 minutes

Cooking Temperature: 350°F (175°C)

Dana Wagtail

Chicken and Pumpkin Soup

Ingredients:

- 2 cups (475 ml) Boneless chicken breast, cooked and shredded
- 1 cup (240 g) pumpkin, diced
- 1/2 cup (120 g) brown rice
- 4 cups (950 ml) low-sodium chicken broth

Steps:

1. Cook chicken and set aside.
2. In a pot, simmer pumpkin, rice, and chicken broth until tender.
3. Add the shredded chicken before serving.

Cooking Time: 25 minutes

Cooking Temperature: Medium Heat.

Chicken and Barley Risotto

Ingredients:

- 2 cups (475 ml) Boneless chicken breast, cooked and diced
- 1 cup (190 g) pearl barley
- 1/2 cup (75 g) butternut squash, diced
- 1/4 cup (60 g) green peas
- 2 cups (475 ml) low-sodium chicken broth

Steps:

1. Cook barley in chicken broth until tender.
2. Add diced chicken, butternut squash, and peas.
3. Simmer until the squash is soft.

Cooking Time: 30 minutes

Cooking Temperature: Medium Heat.

Dana Wagtail

Chicken and Pumpkin Pie

Ingredients:

- 2 cups (475 ml) Boneless chicken breast, cooked and shredded
- 1 cup (240 g) pumpkin, mashed
- 1/2 cup (75 g) oats
- 1/4 cup (60 ml) low-sodium chicken broth

Steps:

1. Mix shredded chicken, mashed pumpkin, oats, and chicken broth.
2. Bake at 350°F (175°C) for 30 minutes.

Cooking Time: 30 minutes

Cooking Temperature: 350°F (175°C)

Chicken and Lentil Soup

Ingredients:

- 2 cups (475 ml) Boneless chicken breast, cooked and diced
- 1 cup (190 g) brown lentils
- 1/2 cup (75 g) carrots, finely chopped
- 1/4 cup (60 g) kale[xi], chopped
- 3 cups (710 ml) low-sodium chicken broth

Steps:

1. Combine cooked chicken, brown lentils, chopped carrots, kale, and chicken broth in a pot.
2. Simmer until lentils are tender.

Cooking Time: 25 minutes

Cooking Temperature: Medium Heat.

[xi] *While rich in nutrients, kale contains oxalic acid. Offer it in moderation to avoid potential issues.*

Dana Wagtail

Chicken and Carrot Omelette

Ingredients:

- 2 cups (475 ml) Boneless chicken breast, cooked and shredded
- 1 cup (240 g) carrots, grated
- 2 eggs
- 1/4 cup (60 ml) low-sodium chicken broth

Steps:

1. Mix shredded chicken, grated carrots, eggs, and chicken broth.
2. Cook as you would an omelette.

Cooking Time: 10 minutes

Cooking Temperature: Medium Heat.

Chicken and Rice Meatballs

Ingredients:

- 2 cups (475 ml) Boneless chicken breast, cooked and minced
- 1 cup (185 g) white rice, cooked
- 1/2 cup (75 g) broccoli florets, finely chopped
- 1/4 cup (60 ml) low-sodium chicken broth

Steps:

1. Combine minced chicken, cooked white rice, chopped broccoli, and chicken broth.
2. Form into meatballs.
3. Bake at 350°F (175°C) for 20 minutes.

Cooking Time: 20 minutes

Cooking Temperature: 350°F (175°C)

Dana Wagtail

Chicken and Butternut Squash Soup

Ingredients:

- 2 cups (475 ml) Boneless chicken breast, cooked and shredded
- 1 cup (240 g) butternut squash, diced
- 1/2 cup (120 g) white rice
- 4 cups (950 ml) low-sodium chicken broth

Steps:

1. Cook chicken and set aside.
2. In a pot, simmer butternut squash, white rice, and chicken broth until tender.
3. Add the shredded chicken before serving.

Cooking Time: 25 minutes

Cooking Temperature: Medium Heat.

Chicken and Potato Pancakes

Ingredients:

- 2 cups (475 ml) Boneless chicken breast, cooked and minced
- 1 cup (200 g) potatoes, grated
- 1/2 cup (75 g) carrots, finely chopped
- 2 eggs

Steps:

1. Mix minced chicken, grated potatoes, chopped carrots, and eggs.
2. Form into small pancakes.
3. Cook until golden brown.

Cooking Time: 10 minutes

Cooking Temperature: Medium Heat.

Dana Wagtail

Chicken and Cheese Pupcakes

Ingredients:

- 1 cup (240 g) Boneless cooked chicken, shredded
- 1 cup (120 g) whole wheat flour
- 1/2 cup (60 g) grated cheddar cheese
- 1 egg
- 1/2 cup (120 ml) water

Steps:

1. Preheat your oven to 350°F (175°C).
2. In a bowl, combine the cooked chicken, whole wheat flour, cheddar cheese, egg, and water.
3. Mix until it forms a batter.
4. Spoon the batter into muffin cups.
5. Bake for approximately 20 minutes until they're firm and golden.

Cooking Time: 20 minutes

Cooking Temperature: 350°F (175°C).

Chicken and Brown Rice Meatloaf

Ingredients:

- 2 cups (475 ml) Boneless chicken breast, cooked and diced
- 1 cup (185 g) brown rice, cooked
- 1/2 cup (75 g) carrots, finely chopped
- 1/4 cup (60 g) green beans, sliced
- 2 tablespoons (30 ml) low-sodium chicken broth

Steps:

1. Combine diced chicken, cooked brown rice, chopped carrots, green beans, and low-sodium chicken broth.
2. Form the mixture into a meatloaf shape.
3. Bake at 350°F (175°C) for 25 minutes.

Cooking Time: 25 minutes

Cooking Temperature: 350°F (175°C).

Dana Wagtail

Chicken and Potato Tacos

Ingredients:

- 2 cups (475 ml) Boneless chicken breast, cooked and shredded
- 1 cup (240 g) potatoes, diced and cooked
- 1/2 cup (75 g) low-fat plain yogurt
- 1/4 cup (60 ml) water
- 1/2 teaspoon (2.5 ml) turmeric

Steps:

1. Mix shredded chicken, cooked diced potatoes, low-fat plain yoghurt, water, and turmeric.
2. Fill small tortillas to create dog-friendly tacos.

Cooking Time: None (cold dish)

Cooking Temperature: Room temperature

Chicken and Green Bean Casserole

Ingredients:

- 2 cups (475 ml) Boneless chicken breast, cooked and shredded
- 1 cup (185 g) green beans, chopped
- 1/2 cup (75 g) potatoes, diced
- 1/4 cup (60 ml) low-sodium chicken broth

Steps:

1. Cook chicken and shred it.
2. Add chopped green beans, diced potatoes, and low-sodium chicken broth.
3. Bake at 375°F (190°C) for 25 minutes.

Cooking Time: 25 minutes

Cooking Temperature: 350°F (175°C).

Chicken and Rice Meatballs

Ingredients:

- 2 cups (475 ml) Boneless chicken breast, cooked and minced
- 1 cup (185 g) white rice, cooked
- 1/2 cup (75 g) green beans, finely chopped
- 1/4 cup (60 ml) low-sodium chicken broth
- 1 egg

Steps:

1. In a bowl, combine the minced chicken, cooked white rice, chopped green beans, low-sodium chicken broth, and the egg.
2. Form the mixture into meatballs.
3. Bake at 350°F (175°C) for 20 minutes.

Cooking Time: 20 minutes

Cooking Temperature: 350°F (175°C).

Chicken and Barley Casserole

Ingredients:

- 2 cups (475 ml) Boneless chicken breast, cooked and shredded
- 1 cup (185 g) pearl barley
- 1/2 cup (75 g) green peas
- 1/4 cup (60 ml) low-sodium chicken broth

Steps:

1. Combine the shredded chicken, pearl barley, green peas, and low-sodium chicken broth.
2. Bake at 350°F (175°C) for 25 minutes.

Cooking Time: 25 minutes

Cooking Temperature: 350°F (175°C).

Chicken and Rice Burritos

Ingredients:

- 2 cups (475 ml) Boneless chicken breast, cooked and shredded
- 1 cup (185 g) white rice, cooked
- 1/2 cup (75 g) black beans, drained and rinsed
- 1/4 cup (60 ml) low-sodium chicken broth
- Whole wheat tortillas

Steps:

1. Mix shredded chicken, cooked white rice, black beans, and low-sodium chicken broth.
2. Use the mixture to fill whole wheat tortillas and make burritos.

Cooking Time: 20 minutes

Cooking Temperature: Medium Heat

Tuna and Spinach Pasta

Ingredients:

- 1 cup (240 g) whole wheat pasta
- 1 can (150 g) tuna in water, drained
- 1 cup (240 g) fresh spinach[xii], chopped

[xii] Spinach is b*est served in moderation. While spinach contains beneficial nutrients, it also has oxalic acid, which can be harmful in large quantities.*

- 1/4 cup (60 ml) low-sodium chicken broth

Steps:

1. Cook pasta according to package Steps.
2. Combine tuna, spinach, and chicken broth in a pan.
3. Mix in cooked pasta.

Cooking Time: 15 minutes

Cooking Temperature: Low Heat.

Salmon and Potato Patties

Ingredients:

- 2 cans (300 g) canned salmon, drained
- 2 cups (475 g) sweet potatoes, mashed
- 1/2 cup (120 g) peas, mashed
- 1/4 cup (60 ml) fish oil

Steps:

1. Combine canned salmon, mashed sweet potatoes, and peas.
2. Form into patties.
3. Bake at 375°F (190°C) for 20 minutes.

Cooking Time: 20 minutes

Cooking Temperature: 375°F (190°C)

Dana Wagtail

Salmon and Asparagus Stir-Fry

Ingredients:

- 2 cups (475 ml) canned salmon, drained
- 1 cup (240 g) asparagus, chopped
- 1/2 cup (75 g) brown rice, cooked
- 1/4 cup (60 ml) fish oil

Steps:

1. Sauté asparagus in fish oil.
2. Add canned salmon and cooked brown rice.
3. Stir-fry until Heated through.

Cooking Time: 15 minutes

Cooking Temperature: Medium Heat.

Tuna and Carrot Muffins

Ingredients:

- 2 cans (300 g) canned tuna, drained
- 1 cup (240 g) carrots, grated
- 1/2 cup (75 g) whole wheat flour
- 2 eggs

Steps:

1. Combine tuna, grated carrots, whole wheat flour, and eggs.
2. Spoon into muffin cups.
3. Bake at 350°F (175°C) for 20 minutes.

Cooking Time: 20 minutes

Cooking Temperature: 350°F (175°C)

Dana Wagtail

Salmon and Sweet Potato Cakes

Ingredients:

- 2 cans (300 g) canned salmon, drained
- 1 cup (200 g) sweet potatoes, mashed
- 1/2 cup (75 g) spinach[xiii], chopped
- 1/4 cup (60 g) oats

Steps:

1. Combine canned salmon, mashed sweet potatoes, chopped spinach, and oats.
2. Form into small cakes.
3. Bake at 350°F (175°C) for 20 minutes.

Cooking Time: 20 minutes

Cooking Temperature: 350°F (175°C)

[xiii] Spinach is b*est served in moderation. While spinach contains beneficial nutrients, it also has oxalic acid, which can be harmful in large quantities*

Tuna and Rice Salad

Ingredients:

- 1 cup (240 g) white rice, cooked
- 1 can (150 g) tuna in water, drained
- 1/2 cup (75 g) peas
- 1/4 cup (60 g) carrots, finely chopped
- 2 tablespoons (30 ml) olive oil

Steps:

1. Mix cooked white rice, drained tuna, peas, chopped carrots, and olive oil.
2. Serve as a salad.

Cooking Time: None (cold salad)

Cooking Temperature: Room temperature

Dana Wagtail

Salmon and Rice Medley

Ingredients:

- 2 cans (300 g) canned salmon, drained
- 1 cup (185 g) white rice, cooked
- 1/2 cup (75 g) carrots, finely chopped
- 1/4 cup (60 ml) fish oil

Steps:

1. Combine canned salmon, cooked white rice, chopped carrots, and fish oil.
2. Mix well.

Cooking Time: None (cold dish)

Cooking Temperature: Room temperature

Tuna and Potato Salad

Ingredients:

- 2 cans (300 g) canned tuna, drained
- 1 cup (240 g) potatoes, diced
- 1/2 cup (75 g) green beans, sliced
- 1/4 cup (60 ml) olive oil

Steps:

1. Mix drained tuna, diced potatoes, sliced green beans, and olive oil.
2. Serve as a salad.

Cooking Time: None (cold salad)

Cooking Temperature: Room temperature

Tuna and Spinach Salad

Ingredients:

- 1 can (150 g) tuna in water, drained
- 1 cup (240 g) fresh spinach[xiv] leaves
- 1/4 cup (60 ml) olive oil
- 1/4 cup (60 ml) water

Steps:

1. Mix drained tuna with fresh spinach leaves.
2. Drizzle olive oil and water over the mixture.
3. Serve as a salad.

Cooking Time: None (cold salad)

Cooking Temperature: Room temperature

[xiv] Spinach is best served in moderation. While spinach contains beneficial nutrients, it also has oxalic acid, which can be harmful in large quantities.

Tuna and Spinach Wrap

Ingredients:

- 2 cans (300 g) canned tuna, drained
- 1 cup (240 g) fresh spinach[xv] leaves
- 1/4 cup (60 ml) low-sodium fish broth
- Whole wheat tortillas

Steps:

1. Combine drained tuna, fresh spinach leaves, and low-sodium fish broth.
2. Use the mixture to fill whole wheat tortillas and create wraps.

Cooking Time: None (cold dish)

Cooking Temperature: Room temperature

[xv] Spinach is b*est served in moderation. While spinach contains beneficial nutrients, it also has oxalic acid, which can be harmful in large quantities.*

Dana Wagtail

Salmon and Rice Medley

Ingredients:

- 2 cans (300 g) canned salmon, drained
- 1 cup (185 g) white rice, cooked
- 1/2 cup (75 g) spinach[xvi], chopped
- 1/4 cup (60 g) fish oil

Steps:

1. Combine canned salmon, cooked white rice, chopped spinach, and fish oil.
2. Mix well.

Cooking Time: None (cold dish)

Cooking Temperature: Room temperature

[xvi] Spinach is b*est served in moderation. While spinach contains beneficial nutrients, it also has oxalic acid, which can be harmful in large quantities*

Salmon and Carrot Omelette

Ingredients:

- 2 cans (300 g) canned salmon, drained
- 1 cup (185 g) carrots, grated
- 2 eggs
- 1/4 cup (60 ml) low-sodium fish broth

Steps:

1. Mix the drained canned salmon, grated carrots, eggs, and low-sodium fish broth.
2. Cook as you would an omelette.

Cooking Time: 10 minutes

Cooking Temperature: Low Heat

Dana Wagtail

Salmon and Quinoa Salad

Ingredients:

- 2 cans (300 g) canned salmon, drained
- 1 cup (185 g) quinoa, cooked
- 1/2 cup (75 g) cucumber, diced
- 1/4 cup (60 ml) low-sodium fish broth

Steps:

1. Combine drained canned salmon, cooked quinoa, diced cucumber, and low-sodium fish broth.
2. Serve as a salad.

Cooking Time: None (cold salad)

Cooking Temperature: Room temperature

Lamb and Rice Medley

Ingredients:

- 2 cups (475 ml) lean ground lamb
- 1 cup (190 g) white rice, cooked
- 1/2 cup (75 g) carrots, finely chopped
- 1/4 cup (60 g) green beans, sliced
- 2 tablespoons (30 ml) olive oil

Steps:

1. Brown ground lamb in a skillet.
2. Add carrots and green beans.
3. Mix in cooked rice and olive oil.

Cooking Time: 20 minutes

Cooking Temperature: Medium Heat.

Dana Wagtail

Lamb and Barley Stew

Ingredients:

- 2 cups (475 ml) lean ground lamb
- 1 cup (190 g) pearl barley
- 1/2 cup (75 g) carrots, diced
- 1/4 cup (60 g) peas
- 3 cups (710 ml) water

Steps:

1. Brown ground lamb in a pot.
2. Add pearl barley, diced carrots, peas, and water.
3. Simmer until barley is tender.

Cooking Time: 30 minutes

Cooking Temperature: Medium Heat.

Lamb and Pea Risotto

Ingredients:

- 2 cups (475 ml) lean ground lamb
- 1 cup (185 g) arborio rice
- 1/2 cup (75 g) green peas
- 1/4 cup (60 ml) low-sodium beef broth

Steps:

1. Brown ground lamb in a pot.
2. Add arborio rice, green peas, and beef broth.
3. Cook, stirring frequently until rice is tender.

Cooking Time: 25 minutes

Cooking Temperature: Medium Heat.

Dana Wagtail

Lamb and Brown Rice Stew

Ingredients:

- 2 cups (475 ml) lean ground lamb
- 1 cup (185 g) brown rice, cooked
- 1/2 cup (75 g) peas
- 1/4 cup (60 g) carrots, finely chopped
- 2 cups (475 ml) low-sodium beef broth

Steps:

1. Brown ground lamb in a pot.
2. Add cooked brown rice, peas, carrots, and beef broth.
3. Simmer until the stew thickens and is Heated through.

Cooking Time: 20 minutes

Cooking Temperature: Medium Heat.

Lamb and Rice Balls

Ingredients:

- 2 cups (475 ml) lean ground lamb
- 1 cup (185 g) white rice, cooked
- 1/2 cup (75 g) peas
- 1/4 cup (60 g) low-sodium lamb broth
- 1 egg

Steps:

1. Brown ground lamb in a skillet.
2. Combine cooked white rice, peas, low-sodium lamb broth, and the egg.
3. Form into small balls.
4. Cook until Heated through.

Cooking Time: 20 minutes

Cooking Temperature: Medium Heat.

Dana Wagtail

Pork and Apple Casserole

Ingredients:

- 2 cups (475 ml) lean ground pork
- 1 cup (200 g) apples[xvii], diced
- 1/2 cup (75 g) broccoli florets
- 1/4 cup (60 ml) water

Steps:

1. Brown ground pork in a pan.
2. Add diced apples, broccoli, and water.
3. Simmer until apples are soft.

Cooking Time: 20 minutes

Cooking Temperature: Medium Heat

[xvii] *Remove seeds and core. Offer in moderation. Apples are a good source of vitamins.*

Pork and Rice Stuffed Peppers

Ingredients:

- 2 cups (475 ml) lean ground pork
- 1 cup (185 g) white rice, cooked
- 1/2 cup (75 g) bell peppers
- 1/4 cup (60 ml) water

Steps:

1. Brown ground pork in a skillet.
2. Mix in cooked white rice.
3. Stuff bell peppers with the mixture and bake at 350°F (175°C) for 30 minutes.

Cooking Time: 30 minutes

Cooking Temperature: 350°F (175°C)

Dana Wagtail

Pork and Rice Stir-Fry

Ingredients:

- 2 cups (475 ml) lean ground pork
- 1 cup (185 g) white rice, cooked
- 1/2 cup (75 g) green bell peppers, sliced

Steps:

1. Brown ground pork in a skillet.
2. Add cooked white rice, and sliced green bell peppers.
3. Stir-fry until Heated through.

Cooking Time: 15 minutes

Cooking Temperature: Medium Heat.

Pork and Spinach Quiche

Ingredients:

- 2 cups (475 ml) lean ground pork
- 1 cup (240 g) fresh spinach[xviii], chopped
- 1/2 cup (75 g) low-fat cottage cheese
- 1/4 cup (60 g) whole wheat pie crust

2 eggs

Steps:

1. Brown ground pork in a skillet.
2. Mix in chopped spinach, low-fat cottage cheese, and eggs.
3. Pour into the whole wheat pie crust and bake at 375°F (190°C) for 25 minutes.

Cooking Time: 25 minutes

Cooking Temperature: 375°F (190°C)

[xviii] Spinach is b*est served in moderation. While spinach contains beneficial nutrients, it also has oxalic acid, which can be harmful in large quantities.*

Dana Wagtail

Pork and Carrot Stew

Ingredients:

- 2 cups (475 ml) lean ground pork
- 1 cup (240 g) carrots, sliced
- 1/2 cup (75 g) brown rice, cooked
- 1/4 cup (60 ml) water

Steps:

1. Brown ground pork in a skillet.
2. Add sliced carrots, cooked brown rice, and water.
3. Simmer until carrots are tender.
4. Allow too cool before serving.

Cooking Time: 20 minutes

Cooking Temperature: Medium Heat.

Pork and Apple Risotto

Ingredients:

- 2 cups (475 ml) lean ground pork
- 1 cup (240 g) apples[xix], diced
- 1/2 cup (75 g) white rice, cooked
- 1/4 cup (60 g) low-sodium chicken broth

Steps:

1. Brown ground pork in a skillet.
2. Add diced apples, cooked white rice, and low-sodium chicken broth.
3. Simmer until the risotto thickens and is Heated through.

Cooking Time: 20 minutes

Cooking Temperature: Medium Heat.

[xix] *Remove seeds and core. Offer in moderation. Apples are a good source of vitamins.*

Dana Wagtail

Pork and Barley Risotto

Ingredients:

- 2 cups (475 ml) lean ground pork
- 1 cup (185 g) pearl barley
- 1/2 cup (75 g) zucchini, diced
- 1/4 cup (60 g) carrots, finely chopped
- 2 cups (475 ml) low-sodium pork broth

Steps:

1. Brown ground pork in a pot.
2. Mix in pearl barley, diced zucchini, carrots, and low-sodium pork broth.
3. Simmer until the risotto thickens and is Heated through.

Cooking Time: 20 minutes

Cooking Temperature: Medium Heat.

Pork and Sweet Potato Casserole

Ingredients:

- 2 cups (475 ml) lean ground pork
- 1 cup (200 g) sweet potatoes, diced and cooked
- 1/2 cup (75 g) green beans, chopped
- 1/4 cup (60 ml) low-sodium pork broth

Steps:

1. Brown ground pork in a skillet.
2. Add cooked sweet potatoes, chopped green beans, and low-sodium pork broth.
3. Bake at 350°F (175°C) for 25 minutes.

Cooking Time: 25 minutes

Cooking Temperature: 350°F (175°C).

Dana Wagtail

Pork and Potato Bake

Ingredients:

- 2 cups (475 ml) lean ground pork
- 1 cup (200 g) potatoes, diced and cooked
- 1/2 cup (75 g) broccoli florets
- 1/4 cup (60 ml) low-sodium pork broth

Steps:

1. Brown the ground pork in a skillet.
2. Add cooked diced potatoes, broccoli florets, and low-sodium pork broth.
3. Bake at 375°F (190°C) for 20 minutes.

Cooking Time: 20 minutes

Cooking Temperature: 350°F (175°C).

Turkey and Quinoa Bowl

Ingredients:

- 2 cups (475 ml) ground turkey
- 1 cup (185 g) quinoa, cooked
- 1/2 cup (75 g) zucchini, grated
- 1/4 cup (60 g) cranberries

Steps:

Dana Wagtail

1. Cook ground turkey in a skillet until browned.
2. Mix in cooked quinoa, grated zucchini, and cranberries.

Cooking Time: 15 minutes

Cooking Temperature: Medium Heat.

Turkey and Lentil Stew

Ingredients:

- 2 cups (475 ml) ground turkey
- 1 cup (190 g) brown lentils
- 1/2 cup (75 g) carrots, sliced
- 1/4 cup (60 g) spinach[xx], chopped
- 3 cups (710 ml) water

Steps:

1. Brown ground turkey in a pot.
2. Add lentils, carrots, spinach, and water.
3. Cook until lentils are tender.

Cooking Time: 25 minutes

Cooking Temperature: Medium Heat.

[xx] Spinach is b*est served in moderation. While spinach contains beneficial nutrients, it also has oxalic acid, which can be harmful in large quantities.*

Dana Wagtail

Turkey and Rice Pilaf

Ingredients:

- 2 cups (475 ml) ground turkey
- 1 cup (185 g) brown rice, cooked
- 1/2 cup (75 g) broccoli florets
- 1/4 cup (60 g) cranberries
- 2 tablespoons (30 ml) olive oil

Steps:

1. Cook ground turkey in a skillet.
2. Mix in cooked brown rice, broccoli, cranberries, and olive oil.

Cooking Time: 20 minutes

Cooking Temperature: Medium Heat.

Turkey and Broccoli Casserole

Ingredients:

- 2 cups (475 ml) ground turkey
- 1 cup (240 g) broccoli florets
- 1/2 cup (75 g) potatoes, diced
- 1/4 cup (60 ml) low-sodium chicken broth

Steps:

1. Brown ground turkey in a skillet.
2. Add broccoli, diced potatoes, and chicken broth.
3. Bake at 375°F (190°C) for 25 minutes.

Cooking Time: 25 minutes

Cooking Temperature: 375°F (190°C)

Dana Wagtail

Turkey and Quinoa Stuffed Peppers

Ingredients:

- 2 cups (475 ml) ground turkey
- 1 cup (185 g) quinoa, cooked
- 1/2 cup (75 g) bell peppers
- 1/4 cup (60 ml) low-sodium chicken broth

Steps:

1. Brown ground turkey in a skillet.
2. Mix in cooked quinoa and chicken broth.
3. Stuff bell peppers with the mixture and bake at 350°F (175°C) for 25 minutes.

Cooking Time: 25 minutes

Cooking Temperature: 350°F (175°C)

Turkey and Spinach Wraps

Ingredients:

- 2 cups (475 ml) ground turkey
- 1 cup (240 g) fresh spinach[xxi] leaves
- 1/2 cup (75 g) low-fat cottage cheese
- 1/4 cup (60 g) whole wHeat tortillas

Steps:

1. Brown ground turkey in a skillet.
2. Mix in fresh spinach and low-fat cottage cheese.
3. Use the mixture to fill whole wHeat tortillas.

Cooking Time: 10 minutes

Cooking Temperature: Medium Heat.

[xxi] *Spinach is best served in moderation. While spinach contains beneficial nutrients, it also has oxalic acid, which can be harmful in large quantities.*

Dana Wagtail

Turkey and Pumpkin Stew

Ingredients:

- 2 cups (475 ml) ground turkey
- 1 cup (200 g) pumpkin, diced
- 1/2 cup (75 g) potatoes, diced
- 1/4 cup (60 ml) low-sodium chicken broth

Steps:

1. Brown ground turkey in a skillet.
2. Add diced pumpkin, potatoes, and chicken broth.
3. Simmer until pumpkin and potatoes are soft.

Cooking Time: 20 minutes

Cooking Temperature: Medium Heat.

Turkey and Pumpkin Stuffed Kong's

Ingredients:

- 1 cup (240 g) ground turkey
- 1/2 cup (75 g) canned pumpkin
- 2 tablespoons (30 ml) plain yogurt

Steps:

1. Cook the ground turkey in a skillet until browned.
2. Mix in canned pumpkin and plain yogurt.
3. Stuff this mixture into Kong's or other treat-dispensing toys for a fun and tasty challenge.

Cooking Time: 20 minutes

Cooking Temperature: Medium Heat.

Dana Wagtail

Turkey and Oatmeal Pancakes

Ingredients:

- 2 cups (475 ml) ground turkey
- 1 cup (185 g) oatmeal
- 1/2 cup (75 g) peas
- 1/4 cup (60 ml) low-sodium chicken broth
- 2 eggs

Steps:

1. Brown ground turkey in a skillet.
2. Combine oatmeal, peas, low-sodium chicken broth, and eggs.
3. Cook as you would pancakes.

Cooking Time: 10 minutes

Cooking Temperature: Medium Heat.

Turkey and Rice Stuffed Tomatoes

Ingredients:

- 2 cups (475 ml) ground turkey
- 1 cup (185 g) white rice, cooked
- 1/2 cup (75 g) tomatoes[xxii]
- 1/4 cup (60 ml) water

Steps:

1. Brown ground turkey in a skillet.
2. Mix in cooked white rice.
3. Hollow out tomatoes and stuff them with the mixture.
4. Bake at 350°F (175°C) for 20 minutes.

Cooking Time: 20 minutes

Cooking Temperature: 375°F (190°C)

[xxii] *Ripe tomatoes are generally safe, green parts and stems contain solanine, which can be toxic. Offer in moderation.*

Dana Wagtail

Turkey and Sweet Potato Hash

Ingredients:

- 2 cups (475 ml) ground turkey
- 1 cup (200 g) sweet potatoes, diced and cooked
- 1/2 cup (75 g) green peas
- 1/4 cup (60 ml) water

Steps:

1. Brown ground turkey in a skillet.
2. Add cooked sweet potatoes, green peas, and water.
3. Cook until Heated through.

Cooking Time: 20 minutes

Cooking Temperature: Medium Heat

Turkey and Carrot Stew

Ingredients:

- 2 cups (475 ml) ground turkey
- 1 cup (185 g) carrots, diced
- 1/2 cup (75 g) brown rice, cooked
- 1/4 cup (60 ml) water

Steps:

1. Brown the ground turkey in a skillet.
2. Add diced carrots, cooked brown rice, and water.
3. Simmer until the stew thickens and is Heated through.

Cooking Time: 20 minutes

Cooking Temperature: Medium Heat

Dana Wagtail

Turkey and Green Bean Stir-Fry

Ingredients:

- 2 cups (475 ml) ground turkey
- 1 cup (185 g) green beans, chopped
- 1/2 cup (75 g) brown rice, cooked
- 1/4 cup (60 ml) low-sodium turkey broth

Steps:

1. Brown the ground turkey in a skillet.
2. Mix in chopped green beans, cooked brown rice, and low-sodium turkey broth.
3. Stir-fry until Heated through.

Cooking Time: 20 minutes

Cooking Temperature: Medium Heat

Turkey and Cranberry Balls

Ingredients:

- 1 cup (240 g) ground turkey
- 1/4 cup (60 ml) unsweetened cranberry juice
- 1/4 cup (60 ml) water

Steps:

1. In a bowl, combine the ground turkey, unsweetened cranberry juice, and water.
2. Form the mixture into small balls and place them on a baking sheet.
3. Bake at 350°F (175°C) for about 15-20 minutes until they're cooked through.

Cooking Time: 15 - 20 minutes

Cooking Temperature: 375°F (190°C)

Veggie and Oatmeal Bake

Ingredients:

- 1 cup (240 g) oats
- 1/2 cup (75 g) sweet potatoes, mashed
- 1/4 cup (60 g) peas
- 1/4 cup (60 g) carrots, finely chopped
- 1/4 cup (60 g) broccoli florets

2 eggs

Steps:

1. Mix oats, mashed sweet potatoes, peas, carrots, and broccoli.
2. Beat eggs and add to the mixture.
3. Bake at 350°F (175°C) for 25 minutes.

Cooking Time: 25 minutes

Cooking Temperature: 350°F (175°C)

Gourmet Pup

Senior recipes

Dana Wagtail

Introduction

The following healthy and nutritious home-cooked meal ideas are for senior dogs. Each recipe has been prepared to provide a well-rounded and healthy meal for your furry friend.

These recipes offer a variety of options to keep your senior dog happy and healthy. Remember to consult with your veterinarian to ensure the meals meet your dog's specific dietary needs and adjust portion sizes according to your dog's age, size and activity level.

Beef and Sweet Potato Stew:

Ingredients:

- Lean Ground Beef: 150g (5.3 oz)
- Sweet Potatoes: 100g (3.5 oz)
- Spinach[xxiii]: 50g (1.75 oz)
- Water: 100ml (3.4 fl oz)

Steps:

1. Brown beef, add diced sweet potatoes and water, simmer until soft.
2. Add spinach and cook until wilted.

Cooking Time: 20 minutes

Cooking Temperature: Medium Heat

[xxiii] Spinach is b*est served in moderation. While spinach contains beneficial nutrients, it also has oxalic acid, which can be harmful in large quantities*

Dana Wagtail

Beef and Barley Stew:

Ingredients:

- Lean Ground Beef: 150g (5.3 oz)
- Barley: 80g (2.8 oz)
- Carrots: 40g (1.4 oz)
- Green Beans: 40g (1.4 oz)

Steps:

1. Brown beef, cook barley, and steam carrots and green beans.
2. Mix all ingredients and serve.

Cooking Time: About 15 minutes

Cooking Temperature: Medium Heat

Beef and Millet Stew:

Ingredients:

- Lean Ground Beef: 150g (5.3 oz)
- Millet: 80g (2.8 oz)
- Peas: 40g (1.4 oz)
- Carrots: 40g (1.4 oz)

Steps:

1. Brown beef, cook millet, steam peas and carrots.
2. Mix all ingredients and serve.

Cooking Time: About 15 minutes

Cooking Temperature: Medium Heat

Dana Wagtail

Beef and Potato Casserole:

Ingredients:

- Lean Ground Beef: 150g (5.3 oz)
- Potatoes: 100g (3.5 oz)
- Spinach[xxiv]: 50g (1.75 oz)
- Low Sodium Beef Broth: 50ml (1.7 fl oz)

Steps:

1. Brown beef, bake potatoes until tender.
2. Mash potatoes, mix with spinach and beef broth.

Cooking Time: About 20 minutes

Cooking Temperature: Medium Heat

[xxiv] Spinach is b*est served in moderation. While spinach contains beneficial nutrients, it also has oxalic acid, which can be harmful in large quantities*

Chicken and Rice Delight:

Ingredients:

- Boneless Chicken: 200g (7 oz)
- White Rice: 100g (3.5 oz)
- Carrots: 50g (1.75 oz)
- Green Beans: 50g (1.75 oz)

Steps:

1. Boil chicken until fully cooked, then shred.
2. Cook rice and vegetables separately.
3. Mix all ingredients and serve.

Cooking Time: 20 minutes

Cooking Temperature: Medium Heat

Dana Wagtail

Chicken and Sweet Potato Casserole:

Ingredients:

- Boneless Chicken: 200g (7 oz)
- Sweet Potatoes: 100g (3.5 oz)
- Peas: 50g (1.75 oz)
- Low Sodium Chicken Broth: 50ml (1.7 fl oz)

Steps:

1. Bake chicken and sweet potatoes until tender.
2. Mash sweet potatoes, shred chicken, mix with peas and chicken broth.

Cooking Time: 20 minutes

Cooking Temperature: Medium Heat

Chicken and Potato Casserole:

Ingredients:

- Boneless Chicken: 200g (7 oz)
- Potatoes: 100g (3.5 oz)
- Green Beans: 50g (1.75 oz)
- Low Sodium Chicken Broth: 50ml (1.7 fl oz)

Steps:

1. Bake chicken and potatoes until tender.
2. Mash potatoes, shred chicken, mix with green beans and chicken broth.

Cooking Time: 30 minutes

Cooking Temperature: Medium Heat

Dana Wagtail

Chicken and Lentil Stew:

Ingredients:

- Boneless Chicken: 200g (7 oz)
- Cooked Lentils: 100g (3.5 oz)
- Broccoli: 50g (1.75 oz)
- Zucchini: 50g (1.75 oz)

Steps:

1. Bake chicken and cook lentils, steam broccoli and zucchini.
2. Mix all ingredients and serve.

Cooking Time: 20 minutes

Cooking Temperature: Medium Heat

Salmon and Asparagus Surprise:

Ingredients:

- Salmon Fillet: 100g (3.5 oz)
- Asparagus: 80g (2.8 oz)
- Quinoa: 40g (1.4 oz)
- Carrots: 40g (1.4 oz)

Steps:

1. Grill salmon until fully cooked.
2. Steam asparagus and carrots, cook quinoa.
3. Mix all ingredients and serve.

Cooking Time: 20 minutes

Cooking Temperature: Medium Heat

Dana Wagtail

Salmon and Quinoa Medley:

Ingredients:

- Salmon Fillet: 100g (3.5 oz)
- Quinoa: 80g (2.8 oz)
- Broccoli: 40g (1.4 oz)
- Zucchini: 40g (1.4 oz)

Steps:

1. Grill salmon until fully cooked.
2. Cook quinoa and steam broccoli and zucchini.
3. Mix all ingredients and serve.

Cooking Time: 20 minutes

Cooking Temperature: Medium Heat

Salmon and Rice Delight:

Ingredients:

- Salmon Fillet: 100g (3.5 oz)
- White Rice: 80g (2.8 oz)
- Carrots: 40g (1.4 oz)
- Green Beans: 40g (1.4 oz)

Steps:

1. Grill salmon until fully cooked.
2. Cook rice and steam carrots and green beans.
3. Mix all ingredients and serve.

Cooking Time: 20 minutes

Cooking Temperature: Medium Heat

Dana Wagtail

Tuna and Brown Rice Medley:

Ingredients:

- Canned Tuna in Water: 100g (3.5 oz)
- Brown Rice: 80g (2.8 oz)
- Pumpkin: 40g (1.4 oz)
- Carrots: 40g (1.4 oz)

Steps:

1. Drain tuna, mix with cooked brown rice.
2. Steam pumpkin and carrots, then blend.
3. Combine all ingredients and serve.

Cooking Time: 20 minutes

Cooking Temperature: Medium Heat

Tuna and Lentil Medley:

Ingredients:

- Canned Tuna in Water: 100g (3.5 oz)
- Cooked Lentils: 80g (2.8 oz)
- Carrots: 40g (1.4 oz)
- Zucchini: 40g (1.4 oz)

Steps:

1. Drain tuna, mix with cooked lentils.
2. Steam carrots and zucchini, then blend.
3. Combine all ingredients and serve.

Cooking Time: 20 minutes

Cooking Temperature: Medium Heat

Dana Wagtail

Tuna and Oatmeal Delight:

Ingredients:

- Canned Tuna in Water: 100g (3.5 oz)
- Oatmeal: 80g (2.8 oz)
- Pumpkin: 40g (1.4 oz)
- Green Beans: 40g (1.4 oz)

Steps:

1. Drain tuna, mix with cooked oatmeal.
2. Steam pumpkin and green beans, then blend.
3. Combine all ingredients and serve.

Cooking Time: 20 minutes

Cooking Temperature: Medium Heat

Pork and Rice Medley:

Ingredients:

- Lean Ground Pork: 150g (5.3 oz)
- Brown Rice: 100g (3.5 oz)
- Spinach[xxv]: 50g (1.75 oz)
- Pumpkin: 50g (1.75 oz)

Steps:

1. Brown pork, cook rice, steam spinach and pumpkin.
2. Mix all ingredients and serve.

Cooking Time: 20 minutes

Cooking Temperature: Medium Heat

[xxv] Spinach is b*est served in moderation. While spinach contains beneficial nutrients, it also has oxalic acid, which can be harmful in large quantities.*

Dana Wagtail

Pork and Barley Medley:

Ingredients:

- Lean Ground Pork: 150g (5.3 oz)
- Barley: 100g (3.5 oz)
- Broccoli: 50g (1.75 oz)
- Zucchini: 50g (1.75 oz)

Steps:

1. Brown pork, cook barley, steam broccoli and zucchini.
2. Mix all ingredients and serve.

Cooking Time: 20 minutes

Cooking Temperature: Medium Heat

Pork and Millet Medley:

Ingredients:

- Lean Ground Pork: 150g (5.3 oz)
- Millet: 80g (2.8 oz)
- Sweet Potatoes: 40g (1.4 oz)
- Green Beans: 40g (1.4 oz)

Steps:

1. Brown pork, cook millet, steam sweet potatoes and green beans.
2. Mix all ingredients and serve.

Cooking Time: 20 minutes

Cooking Temperature: Medium Heat

Dana Wagtail

Turkey and Brown Rice Surprise:

Ingredients:

- Ground Turkey: 150g (5.3 oz)
- Brown Rice: 100g (3.5 oz)
- Peas: 50g (1.75 oz)
- Carrots: 50g (1.75 oz)

Steps:

1. Brown turkey, cook rice, and steam peas and carrots.
2. Mix all ingredients and serve.

Cooking Time: 20 minutes

Cooking Temperature: Medium Heat

Turkey and Spinach Delight:

Ingredients:

- Ground Turkey: 150g (5.3 oz)
- Spinach[xxvi]: 80g (2.8 oz) *
- Brown Rice: 40g (1.4 oz)
- Broccoli: 40g (1.4 oz)

Steps:

1. Brown turkey, cook rice, steam spinach and broccoli.
2. Mix all ingredients and serve.

Cooking Time: 20 minutes

Cooking Temperature: Medium Heat

[xxvi] Spinach is b*est served in moderation. While spinach contains beneficial nutrients, it also has oxalic acid, which can be harmful in large quantities*

Dana Wagtail

Turkey and Quinoa Surprise:

Ingredients:

- Ground Turkey: 150g (5.3 oz)
- Quinoa: 80g (2.8 oz)
- Spinach[xxvii]: 40g (1.4 oz)*
- Sweet Potatoes: 40g (1.4 oz)

Steps:

1. Brown turkey, cook quinoa, steam spinach and sweet potatoes.
2. Mix all ingredients and serve.

Cooking Time: 20 minutes

Cooking Temperature: Medium Heat

[xxvii] Spinach is b*est served in moderation. While spinach contains beneficial nutrients, it also has oxalic acid, which can be harmful in large quantities*

Gourmet Pup

Treats

Dana Wagtail

Beef and Potato Pancakes

Ingredients:

- 2 cups (475 ml) lean ground beef
- 1 cup (240 g) potatoes, grated
- 1/2 cup (75 g) peas
- 1/4 cup (60 ml) low-sodium beef broth
- 2 eggs

Steps:

1. Brown the ground beef in a skillet.
2. Mix in grated potatoes, peas, low-sodium beef broth, and the eggs.
3. Cook until you have pancake-like patties.

Cooking Time: about 15 minutes

Cooking Temperature: Medium Heat

Beef and Cheddar Biscuits

Ingredients:

- 2 cups (240 g) lean ground beef, cooked and crumbled
- 1 cup (120 g) whole wHeat flour
- 1/2 cup (75 g) grated cheddar cheese
- 1/4 cup (60 ml) beef broth

Steps:

1. Preheat your oven to 350°F (175°C).
2. In a bowl, mix the cooked and crumbled beef, whole wHeat flour, grated cheddar cheese, and beef broth.
3. Knead the dough until it's well combined.
4. Roll out the dough and use cookie cutters to create biscuits.
5. Bake for about 25 minutes until they're crispy.

Cooking Time: 25 minutes

Cooking Temperature: 350°F (175°C).

Dana Wagtail

Beef and Cheese Dog Biscuits

Ingredients:

- 2 cups (240 g) whole wHeat flour
- 1 cup (120 g) lean ground beef, cooked and crumbled
- 1/2 cup (60 g) grated cheddar cheese
- 1/4 cup (60 ml) beef broth
- 1 egg

Steps:

1. Preheat your oven to 350°F (175°C).
2. In a bowl, mix the whole wHeat flour, cooked and crumbled beef, grated cheddar cheese, beef broth, and the egg.
3. Knead the dough until it's well mixed.
4. Roll out the dough and cut out biscuit shapes.
5. Place the biscuits on a baking sheet and bake for about 25 minutes until they're crispy.

Cooking Time: 25 minutes

Cooking Temperature: 350°F (175°C).

Beef and Carrot Poppers

Ingredients:

- 1 cup (240 g) lean ground beef, cooked and crumbled
- 1/2 cup (75 g) carrots, finely grated
- 1/4 cup (60 ml) low-sodium beef broth
- 1 1/2 cups (180 g) brown rice flour

Steps:

1. Preheat your oven to 350°F (175°C).
2. In a bowl, combine the cooked and crumbled ground beef, finely grated carrots, low-sodium beef broth, and brown rice flour.
3. Form small balls or poppers and place them on a baking sheet.
4. Bake for about 20-25 minutes until they're golden and firm.

Cooking Time: 20 - 25 minutes

Cooking Temperature: 350°F (175°C).

Beef and Potato Swirls

Ingredients:

- 1 cup (240 g) lean ground beef, cooked and minced
- 1 cup (200 g) potatoes, mashed and cooked
- 1/4 cup (60 ml) low-sodium beef broth
- 1 1/2 cups (180 g) coconut flour

Steps:

1. Preheat your oven to 350°F (175°C).
2. In a bowl, combine the cooked minced beef, mashed potatoes, low-sodium beef broth, and coconut flour.
3. Roll out the dough and cut it into swirl shapes.
4. Place the swirls on a baking sheet and bake for about 20-25 minutes until they're golden and crunchy.

Cooking Time: 20 - 25 minutes

Cooking Temperature: 350°F (175°C).

Beef and Sweet Potato Chews

Ingredients:

- 2 cups (475 ml) lean ground beef
- 1 cup (200 g) sweet potatoes, mashed and cooked
- 1/4 cup (60 ml) low-sodium beef broth
- 1/4 cup (60 ml) water
- 1/4 cup (60 ml) vegetable oil

Steps:

1. Preheat your oven to 350°F (175°C).
2. Brown the ground beef in a skillet.
3. In a bowl, mix the cooked mashed sweet potatoes, low-sodium beef broth, water, and vegetable oil.
4. Combine the beef and sweet potato mixture.
5. Spread it on a baking sheet and bake for 15-20 minutes until it's chewy but firm.
6. Allow it too cool before cutting into chewable portions.

Cooking Time: 15 - 20 minutes

Cooking Temperature: 350°F (175°C).

Dana Wagtail

Beef and Blueberry Chew Bars

Ingredients:

- 2 cups (475 ml) lean ground beef
- 1/2 cup (120 g) blueberries
- 1/4 cup (60 ml) low-sodium beef broth
- 1/4 cup (60 ml) water
- 2 cups (240 g) rice flour

Steps:

1. Preheat your oven to 350°F (175°C).
2. Brown the ground beef in a skillet.
3. In a bowl, mix the blueberries, low-sodium beef broth, water, and rice flour.
4. Combine the browned beef with the blueberry mixture.
5. Spread it in a baking dish and bake for 20-25 minutes until it's chewy.
6. Let it cool before cutting into bars.

Cooking Time: 20 - 25 minutes

Cooking Temperature: 350°F (175°C).

Beef and Carrot Chews

Ingredients:

- 2 cups (475 ml) lean ground beef
- 1 cup (185 g) carrots, finely grated
- 1/4 cup (60 ml) low-sodium beef broth
- 1/4 cup (60 ml) water
- 2 cups (240 g) brown rice flour

Steps:

1. Preheat your oven to 350°F (175°C).
2. Brown the ground beef in a skillet.
3. In a bowl, combine the finely grated carrots, low-sodium beef broth, water, and brown rice flour.
4. Mix in the browned beef.
5. Spread the mixture in a baking dish and bake for about 20-25 minutes until it's chewy.
6. Allow it too cool before cutting into chewable portions.

Cooking Time: 20 - 25 minutes

Cooking Temperature: 350°F (175°C).

Dana Wagtail

Beef and Zucchini Chews

Ingredients:

- 2 cups (475 ml) lean ground beef
- 1 cup (120 g) zucchini, grated
- 1/4 cup (60 ml) low-sodium beef broth
- 1/4 cup (60 ml) water
- 2 cups (240 g) oat flour

Steps:

1. Preheat your oven to 350°F (175°C).
2. Brown the ground beef in a skillet.
3. In a bowl, mix the grated zucchini, low-sodium beef broth, water, and oat flour.
4. Combine the browned beef with the zucchini mixture.
5. Roll out the dough and cut it into chewable pieces.
6. Place them on a baking sheet and bake for about 20-25 minutes until they're chewy.
7. Let them cool before serving.

Cooking Time: 20 - 25 minutes

Cooking Temperature: 350°F (175°C).

Chicken and Blueberry Bites

Ingredients:

- 1 cup (240 g) Boneless chicken breast, cooked and diced
- 1/2 cup (60 g) blueberries
- 1/4 cup (60 ml) low-sodium chicken broth
- 1 1/2 cups (180 g) coconut flour

Steps:

1. Preheat your oven to 350°F (175°C).
2. In a bowl, mix the cooked diced chicken, blueberries, low-sodium chicken broth, and coconut flour.
3. Roll out the dough and cut it into bite-sized pieces.
4. Place the bites on a baking sheet and bake for about 15-20 minutes until they're crunchy.

Cooking Time: 15 - 20 minutes

Cooking Temperature: 350°F (175°C).

Dana Wagtail

Chicken and Blueberry Chew Bars

Ingredients:

- 2 cups (475 ml) Boneless chicken breast, cooked and finely shredded
- 1/2 cup (120 g) blueberries
- 1/4 cup (60 ml) low-sodium chicken broth
- 1/4 cup (60 ml) water
- 2 cups (240 g) brown rice flour

Steps:

1. Preheat your oven to 350°F (175°C).
2. In a bowl, combine the finely shredded chicken, blueberries, low-sodium chicken broth, water, and brown rice flour.
3. Mix until you have a dough.
4. Spread the mixture in a baking dish and bake for about 20-25 minutes until it's chewy.
5. Allow it to cool before cutting into bars.

Cooking Time: 20 - 25 minutes

Cooking Temperature: 350°F (175°C).

Chicken and Brown Rice Chewie's

Ingredients:

- 2 cups (475 ml) Boneless chicken breast, cooked and finely shredded
- 1 cup (185 g) brown rice, cooked
- 1/4 cup (60 ml) low-sodium chicken broth
- 1/4 cup (60 ml) water
- 2 tablespoons (30 ml) molasses

Steps:

1. Preheat your oven to 350°F (175°C).
2. In a bowl, combine the finely shredded chicken, cooked brown rice, low-sodium chicken broth, water, and molasses.
3. Mix the ingredients thoroughly.
4. Spread the mixture evenly on a baking sheet.
5. Bake for 15-20 minutes until the chewie's are set but still chewy.
6. Let them cool before cutting into desired shapes.

Cooking Time: 15 - 20 minutes

Cooking Temperature: 350°F (175°C).

Dana Wagtail

Chicken and Carrot Chew Strips

Ingredients:

- 2 cups (475 ml) Boneless chicken breast, cooked and finely shredded
- 1/2 cup (120 g) carrots, grated
- 1/4 cup (60 ml) low-sodium chicken broth
- 1/4 cup (60 ml) water
- 2 cups (240 g) whole wHeat flour

Steps:

1. Preheat your oven to 350°F (175°C).
2. In a bowl, combine the finely shredded chicken, grated carrots, low-sodium chicken broth, water, and whole wHeat flour.
3. Mix the ingredients until you have a dough.
4. Roll out the dough and cut it into strips.
5. Place the strips on a baking sheet and bake for 15-20 minutes until they're chewy.
6. Let them cool before serving.

Cooking Time: 15 - 20 minutes

Cooking Temperature: 350°F (175°C).

Chicken and Green Bean Chew Bars

Ingredients:

- 2 cups (475 ml) Boneless chicken breast, cooked and finely shredded
- 1 cup (120 g) green beans, finely chopped
- 1/4 cup (60 ml) low-sodium chicken broth
- 1/4 cup (60 ml) water
- 2 cups (240 g) rice flour

Steps:

1. Preheat your oven to 350°F (175°C).
2. In a bowl, combine the finely shredded chicken, chopped green beans, low-sodium chicken broth, water, and rice flour.
3. Mix until you have a dough.
4. Spread the mixture in a baking dish and bake for about 20-25 minutes until it's chewy.
5. Allow it to cool before cutting into bars.

Dana Wagtail

Cooking Time: 20 - 25 minutes

Cooking Temperature: 350°F (175°C).

Chicken and Pea Popsicles

Ingredients:

- 2 cups (475 ml) chicken broth (unsalted)
- 1/2 cup (75 g) cooked peas

Steps:

1. Pour the unsalted chicken broth into ice cube trays.
2. Add a few cooked peas to each cube.
3. *Freeze until solid for a delightful icy treat.*

Cooking Time: No Cooking

Cooking Temperature: Freeze.

Dana Wagtail

Chicken and Carrot Pupcakes

Ingredients:

- 1 cup (240 g) Boneless chicken breast, cooked and shredded
- 1/2 cup (75 g) carrots, grated
- 1/4 cup (60 ml) low-sodium chicken broth
- 1 egg
- 1 cup (120 g) whole wHeat flour

Steps:

1. Preheat your oven to 350°F (175°C).
2. In a bowl, combine the shredded chicken, grated carrots, low-sodium chicken broth, egg, and whole wHeat flour.
3. Fill muffin cups and bake for about 20 minutes until they're golden and firm.

Cooking Time: 20 minutes

Cooking Temperature: 350°F (175°C).

Chicken and Sweet Potato Cookies

Ingredients:

- 1 cup (240 g) Boneless chicken breast, cooked and minced
- 1 cup (120 g) sweet potatoes, mashed and cooked
- 1/4 cup (60 ml) low-sodium chicken broth
- 1 1/2 cups (180 g) oat flour

Steps:

1. Preheat your oven to 350°F (175°C).
2. In a bowl, combine the minced chicken, mashed sweet potatoes, low-sodium chicken broth, and oat flour.
3. Form into cookie shapes and place them on a baking sheet.
4. Bake for about 20 minutes until they're firm and lightly browned.

Cooking Time: 20 minutes

Cooking Temperature: 350°F (175°C).

Dana Wagtail

Chicken and Sweet Potato Squares

Ingredients:

- 2 cups (475 ml) Boneless chicken breast, cooked and finely shredded
- 1 cup (200 g) sweet potatoes, mashed and cooked
- 1/4 cup (60 ml) low-sodium chicken broth
- 1/4 cup (60 ml) water
- 1 1/2 cups (180 g) oat flour

Steps:

1. Preheat your oven to 350°F (175°C).
2. In a bowl, combine the shredded chicken, mashed sweet potatoes, low-sodium chicken broth, water, and oat flour.
3. Mix until you have a dough.
4. Roll out the dough and cut it into squares.
5. Place the squares on a baking sheet and bake for about 15-20 minutes until they're chewy.
6. Let them cool before serving.

Gourmet Pup

Cooking Time: 15 - 20 minutes

Cooking Temperature: 350°F (175°C).

Dana Wagtail

Chicken and Zucchini Biscuits

Ingredients:

- 1 cup (240 g) Boneless chicken breast, cooked and shredded
- 1 cup (120 g) zucchini, grated
- 1/4 cup (60 ml) low-sodium chicken broth
- 1 1/2 cups (180 g) whole wHeat flour

Steps:

1. Preheat your oven to 350°F (175°C).
2. In a bowl, combine the shredded chicken, grated zucchini, low-sodium chicken broth, and whole wHeat flour.
3. Roll out the dough and use cookie cutters to make biscuits.
4. Place the biscuits on a baking sheet and bake for about 25-30 minutes until they're crispy.

Cooking Time: 25 - 30 minutes

Cooking Temperature: 350°F (175°C).

Salmon and Sweet Potato Dog Bites

Ingredients:

- 1 cup (240 g) canned salmon, drained and flaked
- 1/2 cup (120 g) cooked sweet potato, mashed
- 1 egg
- 1/4 cup (60 ml) fish oil
- 1 1/2 cups (180 g) brown rice flour

Steps:

1. Preheat your oven to 350°F (175°C).
2. In a bowl, combine the canned salmon, mashed sweet potato, egg, and fish oil.
3. Gradually add brown rice flour until the mixture forms a dough.
4. Roll the dough into small bite-sized balls.
5. Place them on a baking sheet and bake for approximately 20 minutes until they're firm.

Cooking Time: 20 minutes

Cooking Temperature: 350°F (175°C).

Salmon and Sweet Potato Twists

Ingredients:

- 1 cup (240 g) canned salmon, drained and flaked
- 1 cup (200 g) sweet potatoes, mashed and cooked
- 1/4 cup (60 ml) low-sodium fish broth
- 1 1/2 cups (180 g) oat flour

Steps:

1. Preheat your oven to 350°F (175°C).
2. In a bowl, mix the drained canned salmon, mashed sweet potatoes, low-sodium fish broth, and oat flour.
3. Roll the dough into long ropes and twist them.
4. Place them on a baking sheet and bake for about 20 minutes until they're crunchy.

Cooking Time: 20 minutes

Cooking Temperature: 350°F (175°C).

Salmon and Quinoa Muffins

Ingredients:

- 2 cans (300 g) canned salmon, drained
- 1 cup (185 g) quinoa, cooked
- 1/4 cup (60 ml) low-sodium fish broth
- 2 eggs

Steps:

1. Preheat your oven to 350°F (175°C).
2. In a bowl, mix the drained canned salmon, cooked quinoa, low-sodium fish broth, and eggs.
3. Spoon the mixture into muffin cups and bake for about 20-25 minutes until they're set and lightly browned.

Cooking Time: 20 - 25 minutes

Cooking Temperature: 350°F (175°C).

Dana Wagtail

Salmon and Spinach Chew Bars

Ingredients:

- 1 can (150 g) salmon in water, drained and flaked
- 1/2 cup (120 g) fresh spinach[xxviii] leaves
- 1/4 cup (60 ml) low-sodium fish broth
- 1/4 cup (60 ml) water
- 2 cups (240 g) brown rice flour

Steps:

1. Preheat your oven to 350°F (175°C).
2. In a blender, combine the drained flaked salmon, fresh spinach leaves, low-sodium fish broth, water, and brown rice flour until you have a dough.
3. Spread the dough evenly in a baking dish.
4. Bake for 15-20 minutes until it's chewy but firm.
5. Allow it to cool before cutting into chewable bars.

[xxviii] Spinach is b*est served in moderation. While spinach contains beneficial nutrients, it also has oxalic acid, which can be harmful in large quantities.*

Gourmet Pup

Cooking Time: 15 - 20 minutes

Cooking Temperature: 350°F (175°C).

Dana Wagtail

Salmon and Spinach Squares

Ingredients:

- 1 can (150 g) canned salmon, drained and flaked
- 1/2 cup (120 g) fresh spinach[xxix] leaves
- 1/4 cup (60 ml) low-sodium fish broth
- 1 1/2 cups (180 g) oat flour

Steps:

1. Preheat your oven to 350°F (175°C).
2. In a blender, combine the drained flaked salmon, fresh spinach leaves, low-sodium fish broth, and oat flour until you have a dough.
3. Roll out the dough and cut it into squares.
4. Place the squares on a baking sheet and bake for about 15-20 minutes until they're crispy.

Cooking Time: 15 - 20 minutes

Cooking Temperature: 350°F (175°C).

[xxix] Spinach is b*est served in moderation. While spinach contains beneficial nutrients, it also has oxalic acid, which can be harmful in large quantities.*

Tuna and Spinach Chew Squares

Ingredients:

- 1 can (150 g) tuna in water, drained and flaked
- 1/2 cup (120 g) fresh spinach[xxx] leaves
- 1/4 cup (60 ml) low-sodium fish broth
- 1/4 cup (60 ml) water
- 2 cups (240 g) brown rice flour

Steps:

1. Preheat your oven to 350°F (175°C).
2. In a blender, combine the drained flaked tuna, fresh spinach leaves, low-sodium fish broth, water, and brown rice flour until you have a dough.
3. Roll out the dough and cut it into chewable squares.
4. Place them on a baking sheet and bake for 15-20 minutes until they're chewy but firm.
5. Let them cool before serving.

[xxx] Spinach is b*est served in moderation. While spinach contains beneficial nutrients, it also has oxalic acid, which can be harmful in large quantities.*

Dana Wagtail

Cooking Time: 15 - 20 minutes

Cooking Temperature: 350°F (175°C).

Tuna and Spinach Chew Strips

Ingredients:

- 1 can (150 g) tuna in water, drained and flaked
- 1/2 cup (120 g) fresh spinach[xxxi] leaves
- 1/4 cup (60 ml) low-sodium fish broth
- 1/4 cup (60 ml) water
- 2 cups (240 g) rice flour

Steps:

1. Preheat your oven to 350°F (175°C).
2. In a blender, combine the drained flaked tuna, fresh spinach leaves, low-sodium fish broth, water, and rice flour until you have a dough.
3. Roll out the dough and cut it into strips.
4. Place them on a baking sheet and bake for about 15-20 minutes until they're chewy.
5. Let them cool before serving.

[xxxi] Spinach is b*est served in moderation. While spinach contains beneficial nutrients, it also has oxalic acid, which can be harmful in large quantities.*

Dana Wagtail

Cooking Time: 15 - 20 minutes

Cooking Temperature: 350°F (175°C).

Tuna and Spinach Drops

Ingredients:

- 1 can (150 g) tuna in water, drained and flaked
- 1/2 cup (120 g) fresh spinach[xxxii] leaves
- 1/4 cup (60 ml) low-sodium fish broth
- 1 1/2 cups (180 g) oat flour

Steps:

1. Preheat your oven to 350°F (175°C).
2. In a blender, combine the drained flaked tuna, fresh spinach leaves, low-sodium fish broth, and oat flour until you have a dough.
3. Roll the dough into small drops.
4. Place them on a baking sheet and bake for about 15-20 minutes until they're crunchy.

Cooking Time: 15 - 20 minutes

Cooking Temperature: 350°F (175°C).

[xxxii] *Spinach is best served in moderation. While spinach contains beneficial nutrients, it also has oxalic acid, which can be harmful in large quantities*

Dana Wagtail

Tuna and Spinach Popsicles

Ingredients:

- 2 cans (300 g) canned tuna, drained
- 1 cup (240 g) fresh spinach[xxxiii] leaves
- 1/4 cup (60 ml) low-sodium fish broth

Steps:

1. In a blender, combine the drained tuna, fresh spinach leaves, and low-sodium fish broth.
2. Pour the mixture into ice cube trays and freeze until solid.
3. These popsicles are perfect for hot days.

Cooking Time: No Cooking

Cooking Temperature: Freeze.

[xxxiii] Spinach is best served in moderation. While spinach contains beneficial nutrients, it also has oxalic acid, which can be harmful in large quantities

Pork and Apple Cookies

Ingredients:

- 2 cups (475 ml) lean ground pork, cooked and crumbled
- 1 cup (120 g) apples[xxxiv], finely chopped
- 1/4 cup (60 ml) low-sodium pork broth
- 1 1/2 cups (180 g) oat flour

Steps:

1. Preheat your oven to 350°F (175°C).
2. In a bowl, combine the cooked and crumbled ground pork, chopped apples, low-sodium pork broth, and oat flour.
3. Form into cookie shapes and place them on a baking sheet.
4. Bake for about 20 minutes until they're crispy.

Cooking Time: 20 minutes

Cooking Temperature: 350°F (175°C).

[xxxiv] *Remove seeds and core. Offer in moderation. Apples are a good source of vitamins.*

Dana Wagtail

Pork and Apple Chewies

Ingredients:

- 2 cups (475 ml) lean ground pork
- 1/2 cup (120 g) apples[xxxv], finely chopped
- 1/4 cup (60 ml) low-sodium pork broth
- 1/4 cup (60 ml) water
- 2 cups (240 g) coconut flour

Steps:

1. Preheat your oven to 350°F (175°C).
2. Brown the ground pork in a skillet.
3. In a bowl, mix the finely chopped apples, low-sodium pork broth, water, and coconut flour.
4. Combine the browned pork with the apple mixture.
5. Spread it on a baking sheet and bake for 20-25 minutes until it's chewy.
6. Let it cool before cutting into chewable pieces.

Cooking Time: 20 - 25 minutes

Cooking Temperature: 350°F (175°C).

[xxxv] *Remove seeds and core. Offer in moderation. Apples are a good source of vitamins.*

Pork and Apple Doughnuts

Ingredients:

- 1 cup (240 g) lean ground pork, cooked and crumbled
- 1/2 cup (60 g) apples[xxxvi], finely chopped
- 1/4 cup (60 ml) low-sodium pork broth
- 1 1/2 cups (180 g) rice flour

Steps:

1. Preheat your oven to 350°F (175°C).
2. In a bowl, combine the cooked and crumbled ground pork, finely chopped apples, low-sodium pork broth, and rice flour.
3. Form into doughnut shapes.
4. Place them on a baking sheet and bake for about 20-25 minutes until they're crispy.

Cooking Time: 20 - 25 minutes

Cooking Temperature: 350°F (175°C).

[xxxvi] *Remove seeds and core. Offer in moderation. Apples are a good source of vitamins.*

Dana Wagtail

Pork and Blueberry Chew Strips

Ingredients:

- 2 cups (475 ml) lean ground pork
- 1/2 cup (120 g) blueberries
- 1/4 cup (60 ml) low-sodium pork broth
- 1/4 cup (60 ml) water
- 2 cups (240 g) rice flour

Steps:

1. Preheat your oven to 350°F (175°C).
2. Brown the ground pork in a skillet.
3. In a bowl, mix the blueberries, low-sodium pork broth, water, and rice flour.
4. Combine the browned pork with the blueberry mixture.
5. Roll out the dough and cut it into strips.
6. Place them on a baking sheet and bake for about 15-20 minutes until they're chewy.
7. Let them cool before serving.

Cooking Time: 15 - 20 minutes

Cooking Temperature: 350°F (175°C).

Pork and Oatmeal Cookies

Ingredients:

- 2 cups (475 ml) lean ground pork
- 1 cup (120 g) oatmeal
- 1/2 cup (75 g) apple[xxxvii], finely chopped
- 1/4 cup (60 ml) low-sodium pork broth
- 1 egg

Steps:

1. Brown the ground pork in a skillet.
2. Combine oatmeal, chopped apples, low-sodium pork broth, and the egg.
3. Form into cookie shapes.
4. Bake at 350°F (175°C) for 15 minutes.

Cooking Time: 15 minutes

Cooking Temperature: 350°F (175°C).

[xxxvii] *Remove seeds and core. Offer in moderation. Apples are a good source of vitamins.*

Dana Wagtail

Pork and Sweet Potato Chew Strip

Ingredients:

- 2 cups (475 ml) lean ground pork
- 1/2 cup (120 g) sweet potatoes, mashed and cooked
- 1/4 cup (60 ml) low-sodium pork broth
- 1/4 cup (60 ml) water
- 2 cups (240 g) coconut flour

Steps:

1. Preheat your oven to 350°F (175°C).
2. Brown the ground pork in a skillet.
3. In a bowl, mix the mashed cooked sweet potatoes, low-sodium pork broth, water, and coconut flour.
4. Combine the browned pork with the sweet potato mixture.
5. Roll out the dough and cut it into strips.
6. Place them on a baking sheet and bake for 20-25 minutes until they're chewy.
7. Let them cool before serving.

Cooking Time: 20 - 25 minutes

Cooking Temperature: 350°F (175°C).

Pork and Pumpkin Chew Bars

Ingredients:

- 2 cups (475 ml) lean ground pork
- 1 cup (120 g) canned pumpkin
- 1/4 cup (60 ml) low-sodium pork broth
- 1/4 cup (60 ml) water
- 2 cups (240 g) oat flour

Steps:

1. Preheat your oven to 350°F (175°C).
2. Brown the ground pork in a skillet.
3. In a bowl, combine the canned pumpkin, low-sodium pork broth, water, and oat flour.
4. Mix in the browned pork.
5. Spread the mixture in a baking dish and bake for about 20-25 minutes until it's chewy.
6. Allow it to cool before cutting into bars.

Cooking Time: 20 - 25 minutes

Cooking Temperature: 350°F (175°C).

Dana Wagtail

Turkey and Broccoli Muffins

Ingredients:

- 2 cups (475 ml) ground turkey
- 1 cup (185 g) broccoli florets, finely chopped
- 1/2 cup (75 g) whole wHeat flour
- 2 eggs

Steps:

1. Brown ground turkey in a skillet.
2. Combine finely chopped broccoli, whole wHeat flour, and eggs.
3. Spoon into muffin cups and bake at 350°F (175°C) for 20 minutes.

Cooking Time: 20 minutes

Cooking Temperature: 350°F (175°C)

Turkey and Cranberry Dog Jerky

Ingredients:

- 1 lb (450 g) ground turkey
- 1/4 cup (60 ml) unsweetened cranberry juice
- 1 tablespoon (15 ml) olive oil

Steps:

1. Preheat your oven to 170°F (75°C).
2. In a mixing bowl, combine the ground turkey, unsweetened cranberry juice, and olive oil.
3. Spread the mixture evenly on a baking sheet lined with parchment paper.
4. Bake for about 3-4 hours until the turkey jerky is dried and tough.
5. Once cooled, cut it into strips or bite-sized pieces.

Cooking Time: 23 - 4 Hours

Cooking Temperature: 170°F (75°C).

Dana Wagtail

Turkey and Sweet Potato Dog Chews

Ingredients:

- 1 cup (240 g) cooked and mashed sweet potatoes
- 1 cup (240 g) lean ground turkey
- 1/4 cup (60 ml) water

Steps:

1. Preheat your oven to 350°F (175°C).
2. In a bowl, mix the mashed sweet potatoes, lean ground turkey, and water.
3. Roll the mixture into small chews.
4. Place them on a baking sheet and bake for about 25 minutes until they're firm.

Cooking Time: 25 minutes

Cooking Temperature: 350°F (175°C).

Turkey and Cranberry Dog Bar

Ingredients:

- 1 cup (240 g) ground turkey, cooked and minced
- 1/2 cup (60 g) dried cranberries, chopped
- 1 cup (120 g) whole wHeat flour
- 1/4 cup (60 ml) water
- 1 egg

Steps:

1. Preheat your oven to 350°F (175°C).
2. In a bowl, combine the cooked minced turkey, chopped dried cranberries, whole wHeat flour, water, and the egg.
3. Spread the mixture in a baking dish and bake for about 20-25 minutes until it's firm.
4. Cut into bars or squares.

Cooking Time: 20 - 25 minutes

Cooking Temperature: 350°F (175°C).

Dana Wagtail

Turkey and Pumpkin Muffins

Ingredients:

- 1 cup (240 g) ground turkey, cooked and crumbled
- 1/2 cup (120 g) canned pumpkin
- 1/4 cup (60 ml) water
- 1 1/2 cups (180 g) brown rice flour

Steps:

1. Preheat your oven to 350°F (175°C).
2. In a bowl, mix the cooked and crumbled ground turkey, canned pumpkin, water, and brown rice flour.
3. Spoon the mixture into muffin cups.
4. Bake for about 20-25 minutes until they're firm.

Cooking Time: 20 - 25 minutes

Cooking Temperature: 350°F (175°C).

Turkey and Green Bean Chewie's

Ingredients:

- 2 cups (475 ml) ground turkey
- 1/2 cup (120 g) green beans, finely chopped
- 1/4 cup (60 ml) low-sodium turkey broth
- 1/4 cup (60 ml) water
- 2 cups (240 g) oat flour

Steps:

1. Preheat your oven to 350°F (175°C).
2. Brown the ground turkey in a skillet.
3. In a bowl, combine the finely chopped green beans, low-sodium turkey broth, water, and oat flour.
4. Mix in the browned turkey.
5. Spread it on a baking sheet and bake for 20-25 minutes until it's chewy.
6. Let it cool before cutting into chewable pieces.

Cooking Time: 20 - 25 minutes

Cooking Temperature: 350°F (175°C).

Dana Wagtail

Turkey and Cranberry Chunks

Ingredients:

- 2 cups (475 ml) ground turkey
- 1/2 cup (60 g) dried cranberries, chopped
- 1/4 cup (60 ml) low-sodium turkey broth
- 1/4 cup (60 ml) water
- 2 cups (240 g) coconut flour

Steps:

1. Preheat your oven to 350°F (175°C).
2. Brown the ground turkey in a skillet.
3. In a bowl, mix the chopped dried cranberries, low-sodium turkey broth, water, and coconut flour.
4. Combine the browned turkey with the cranberry mixture.
5. Roll out the dough and cut it into chunks.
6. Place them on a baking sheet and bake for about 15-20 minutes until they're chewy.
7. Let them cool before serving.

Cooking Time: 15 - 20 minutes

Cooking Temperature: 350°F (175°C).

Turkey and Spinach Chewie's

Ingredients:

- 2 cups (475 ml) ground turkey
- 1/2 cup (120 g) fresh spinach[xxxviii] leaves
- 1/4 cup (60 ml) low-sodium turkey broth
- 1/4 cup (60 ml) water
- 2 cups (240 g) coconut flour

Steps:

1. Preheat your oven to 350°F (175°C).
2. Brown the ground turkey in a skillet.
3. In a blender, combine the fresh spinach leaves, low-sodium turkey broth, water, and coconut flour until you have a dough.
4. Mix in the browned turkey.
5. Roll out the dough and cut it into chewy pieces.
6. Place them on a baking sheet and bake for about 15-20 minutes until they're chewy.
7. Let them cool before serving.

[xxxviii] Spinach is b*est served in moderation. While spinach contains beneficial nutrients, it also has oxalic acid, which can be harmful in large quantities.*

Dana Wagtail

Cooking Time: 15 - 20 minutes

Cooking Temperature: 350°F (175°C).

Turkey and Pumpkin Chew Bars

Ingredients:

- 2 cups (475 ml) ground turkey
- 1/2 cup (120 g) canned pumpkin
- 1/4 cup (60 ml) low-sodium turkey broth
- 1/4 cup (60 ml) water
- 2 cups (240 g) oat flour

Steps:

1. Preheat your oven to 350°F (175°C).
2. Brown the ground turkey in a skillet.
3. In a bowl, combine the canned pumpkin, low-sodium turkey broth, water, and oat flour.
4. Mix in the browned turkey.
5. Spread the mixture in a baking dish and bake for 20-25 minutes until it's chewy.
6. Allow it to cool before cutting into bars.

Cooking Time: 20 - 25 minutes

Cooking Temperature: 350°F (175°C).

Dana Wagtail

Veggie and Peanut Butter Dog Treats

Ingredients:

- 1 cup (120 g) whole wHeat flour
- 1/2 cup (65 g) carrots, grated
- 1/4 cup (60 ml) natural peanut butter
- 1/4 cup (60 ml) water
- 1 egg

Steps:

1. Preheat your oven to 350°F (175°C).
2. In a mixing bowl, combine whole wheat flour, grated carrots, peanut butter, water, and the egg.
3. Mix until a dough forms.
4. Roll out the dough and use cookie cutters to create fun shapes.
5. Place the treats on a baking sheet and bake for about 20 minutes or until they're golden brown.

Cooking Time: 20 minutes

Cooking Temperature: 350°F (175°C).

Banana and Oatmeal Dog Treats

Ingredients:

- 2 ripe bananas
- 1 cup (80 g) rolled oats
- 1/4 cup (60 ml) unsweetened apple sauce[xxxix]

Steps:

1. Preheat your oven to 350°F (175°C).
2. In a mixing bowl, mash the ripe bananas.
3. Stir in the rolled oats and unsweetened applesauce until you have a dough-like consistency.
4. Drop spoonful's of the mixture onto a baking sheet.
5. Bake for about 15 minutes until the treats are firm and slightly golden.

Cooking Time: 15 minutes

Cooking Temperature: 350°F (175°C).

[xxxix] *Remove seeds and core. Offer in moderation. Apples are a good source of vitamins*

Dana Wagtail

Pumpkin and Cinnamon Dog Biscuits

Ingredients:

- 2 1/2 cups (300 g) whole wHeat flour
- 1/2 cup (120 g) canned pumpkin
- 2 eggs
- 1/2 teaspoon (2.5 ml) cinnamon
- 1/2 teaspoon (2.5 ml) salt

Steps:

1. Preheat your oven to 350°F (175°C).
2. In a bowl, mix the whole wHeat flour, canned pumpkin, eggs, cinnamon, and salt.
3. Knead the dough until it's smooth.
4. Roll out the dough and cut it into biscuit shapes.
5. Place the biscuits on a baking sheet and bake for about 25 minutes until they're golden brown.

Cooking Time: 25 minutes

Cooking Temperature: 350°F (175°C).

Blueberry and Banana Frozen Treats

Ingredients:

- 1 ripe banana
- 1 cup (120 g) blueberries
- 1/2 cup (120 ml) plain yogurt

Steps:

1. In a blender, combine the ripe banana, blueberries, and plain yogurt.
2. Blend until smooth.
3. Pour the mixture into ice cube trays and freeze until solid.
4. These treats are perfect for a refreshing snack on a hot day.

Cooking Time: No Cooking

Cooking Temperature: Freeze

Dana Wagtail

Carrot and Apple Dog Cookies

Ingredients:

- 1 cup (120 g) grated carrots
- 1 cup (240 g) unsweetened apple sauce[xl]
- 1 1/2 cups (180 g) oat flour

Steps:

1. Preheat your oven to 350°F (175°C).
2. In a bowl, mix the grated carrots and unsweetened applesauce.
3. Gradually add the oat flour until you have a dough.
4. Roll out the dough and use cookie cutters to make cookies.
5. Place the cookies on a baking sheet and bake for about 15-20 minutes.

Cooking Time: 15 - 20 minutes

Cooking Temperature: 350°F (175°C).

[xl] *Remove seeds and core. Offer in moderation. Apples are a good source of vitamins*

Peanut Butter and Banana Frozen Treats

Ingredients:

- 1 ripe banana
- 1/4 cup (60 ml) natural peanut butter
- 1/4 cup (60 ml) plain yogurt

Steps:

1. In a bowl, mash the ripe banana.
2. Stir in the natural peanut butter and plain yogurt.
3. Spoon the mixture into ice cube trays and freeze until solid.
4. A refreshing treat for your pup.

Cooking Time: No Cooking

Cooking Temperature: Freeze

Dana Wagtail

Blueberry and Yogurt Frozen Bites

Ingredients:

- 1 cup (120 g) blueberries
- 1/2 cup (120 ml) plain yogurt
- 1/4 cup (60 ml) water

Steps:

1. In a blender, mix the blueberries, plain yogurt, and water until smooth.
2. Pour the mixture into ice cube trays and freeze until solid.
3. A cool and nutritious treat for your furry friend.

Cooking Time: No Cooking

Cooking Temperature: Freeze

Portion Sizes

Puppies

Portion sizes for puppies can vary depending on their age, breed, and activity level. It's essential to consult with your veterinarian to determine the exact portion sizes for your specific puppy.

However, as a general guideline, you can start with the following portion sizes based on your puppy's weight:

1. **Small Breeds (up to 10 pounds / 4.5 kilograms):**
   - 60 to 120 grams of food per meal (1/4 to 1/2 cup)

2. **Medium Breeds (10 - 30 pounds / 4.5 - 13.5 kilograms):**
   - 120 to 240 grams of food per meal (1/2 to 1 cup)

3. **Large Breeds (30 - 60 pounds / 13.5 - 27 kilograms):**
   - 240 to 360 grams of food per meal (1 to 1.5 cups)

4. **Giant Breeds (60+ pounds / 27+ kilograms):**
   - 360 to 480 grams of food per meal (1.5 to 2 cups)

Keep in mind that these are rough estimates, and it's crucial to monitor your puppy's weight and adjust portion sizes accordingly. Puppies are growing rapidly, so you may need to increase their food as they get older. Additionally, the type of food and its caloric content will also have an impact on portion sizes. Always follow your veterinarian's recommendations to ensure your puppy's nutritional needs are met.

Adult Dogs

Determining the appropriate portion size for your dog's meals is crucial to ensure they receive the right amount of nutrients and maintain a healthy weight. Portion sizes can vary depending on your dog's size, age, activity level, and overall health. Here are some general guidelines for weight-appropriate portion sizes for the dog recipes mentioned earlier:

1. **Portion size**

   - Small Breeds (e.g., Chihuahua, Pomeranian): 60 to 120 grams of food per meal (1/4 to 1/2 cup)
   - Medium Breeds (e.g., Beagle, Cocker Spaniel): 120 to 240 grams of food per meal (1/2 to 1 cup).
   - Large Breeds (e.g., Labrador Retriever, Golden Retriever): 240 to 480 grams of food per meal (1.5 to 2 cups).
   - Giant Dogs (Over 45 kg or 100 lbs): 480 to 600 grams of food per meal (2 to 2.5 cups),

2. **Treat Bars :**

   - You should give these treats sparingly.
     - Small breeds - One or two bars
     - Medium breeds - up to four bars
     - Large and XL breeds - up to six bars during training or as occasional rewards.

3. **Treat Twists:**
   - These are treats and should be given sparingly.
     - Small breeds - One or two
     - Medium breeds - up to four twists
     - Large and XL breeds - up to six twists during training or as occasional rewards.

Remember that these are general guidelines, and your dog's specific portion size may differ.

It's important to monitor your dog's weight and adjust portion sizes as needed. Factors such as metabolism, activity level, age, and any underlying health conditions can affect their dietary needs. It's crucial to monitor your dog's weight and adjust portion sizes accordingly.

Consult with your veterinarian to determine the best portion sizes for your dog based on their individual needs, and consider factors such as age, breed, and any underlying health conditions.

Always provide fresh water for your dog, and if you notice any sudden changes in their weight or appetite, consult with your vet for further guidance.

Senior Dogs

Portion sizes for your senior dog should be based on their weight, age, and activity level.

As a general guideline, you can start with the following portion sizes, but it's essential to consult with your veterinarian to determine the exact amount that suits your dog's specific needs.

1. **Small Dogs (Up to 10 kg or 22 lbs):**
    - 60 to 120 grams of food per meal (1/4 to 1/2 cup) depending on activity level.

2. **Medium Dogs (10-25 kg or 22-55 lbs):**
    - 120 to 240 grams of food per meal (1/2 to 1 cup), depending on activity level.

3. **Large Dogs (25-45 kg or 55-100 lbs):**
    - 240 to 480 grams of food per meal (1.5 to 2 cups), depending on activity level.

4. **Giant Dogs (Over 45 kg or 100 lbs):**
    - 480 to 600 grams of food per meal (2 to 2.5 cups), depending on activity level.

Please keep in mind that these are rough estimates, and individual dogs may require more or less food.

Factors such as metabolism, age, and any underlying health conditions can affect their dietary needs. It's crucial to monitor your dog's weight and adjust portion sizes accordingly.

Always consult with your veterinarian to create a tailored feeding plan that meets your senior dog's specific requirements.

www.ingramcontent.com/pod-product-compliance
Lightning Source LLC
LaVergne TN
LVHW052254070426
835507LV00035B/2452